MW00989862

BOUNDARIES FOR LEADERS

ALSO BY DR. HENRY CLOUD

Integrity: The Courage to Meet the Demands of Reality

Necessary Endings: The Employees, Businesses, and Relationships That All of Us Have to Give Up in Order to Move Forward

9 Things You Simply Must Do to Succeed in Love and Life

BOUNDARIES FOR LEADERS

RESULTS, RELATIONSHIPS, AND BEING RIDICULOUSLY IN CHARGE

DR. HENRY CLOUD

HARPER
BUSINESS

An Imprint of HarperCollins*Publishers*
www.harpercollins.com

 For information, address HarperCollins Publishers, 10 East 53rd Street, New York, NY 10022.

HarperCollins books may be purchased for educational, business, or sales promotional use. For information, please e-mail the Special Markets Department at SPsales@harpercollins.com.

FIRST EDITION

Library of Congress Cataloging-in-Publication Data has been applied for.

ISBN: 978-0-06-220633-6

13 14 15 16 17 OV/RRD 10 9 8 7 6 5 4 3 2

This book is dedicated to my clients, with gratitude,
for giving me the privilege of working with you.
You are an awesome bunch,
and I am always inspired by all you do.

ACKNOWLEDGMENTS

There is always a lot that goes into the writing of a book, a great deal of which is the help you get from others. I would like to thank several people for helping this book come to fruition:

First of all, as I said in the dedication, I must acknowledge my clients. You are incredible, and never cease to amaze me with your courage, growth, talents, and accomplishments. As the pages of this book show, you teach me every day, and I love every minute of working with you.

My agents, Jan Miller and Shannon Marven, are the wind in the sails of every project. They keep it moving across the finish line, and are the bridge that helps ideas get to bookshelves or, more accurately nowadays, e-readers. Thanks once again!

My assistant, Alexis Randall, who juggles a lot of activity and creates time out of a hat. Thanks for helping me get it all done, and for the care you show to everyone we work with.

My publisher, Hollis Heimbouch, who is a quadruple threat: painless, yet great editor; experienced publisher; personal-growth devotee; and maven of business content. You are a great match for everything this book needs.

My family, who bring me constant joy, even when wrestling with a manuscript is not so much fun. Thanks for cheering me up on those marathons.

And finally, my spiritual partners who regularly pray for me . . . thank you, and please don't stop!

CONTENTS

Preface *xiii*

CHAPTER 1 The People Are the Plan *1*

CHAPTER 2 Ridiculously in Charge *13*

CHAPTER 3 Leading So Brains Can Work *25*

CHAPTER 4 The Emotional Climate That Makes Brains Perform *51*

CHAPTER 5 Power Through Connection *77*

CHAPTER 6 The Gatekeeper of Thinking *99*

CHAPTER 7 Control and Results *125*

CHAPTER 8 High-Performance Teams *153*

CHAPTER 9 Trust Makes Teams Able to Perform *167*

CHAPTER 10 Boundaries for Yourself *197*

Conclusion *233*

Index *239*

PREFACE

To get results, leadership matters. Leadership matters for an entire organization, and it matters in smaller contexts such as in teams or departments. Because of that, we often talk about leadership disciplines that are essential to creating results and making it all work—disciplines such as casting a vision, shaping the future, developing strategy, engaging the right talent in the right places, fostering innovation and agility, execution, and more. As you know, all of these leadership competencies must be in place for a vision to become a reality.

But . . . there is another truth. Leaders lead *people*, and it is the people who get it all done. And to get it done, they have to be led in a way that they can actually perform, and use all of their horsepower. Said another way, *their brains need to work*. You can cast a great vision, get the right talent, and yet be leading in ways that people's brains literally cannot follow, or sometimes even make work, much less their hearts.

I learned this when I began practice as a clinician. My first job was in a leadership consulting firm, as they wanted a clinician to work with leaders to help them with their personal and interpersonal leadership style to become more effective in leading people. As a result, I fell in love with the topic of leadership, as it relates to the people side of the equation. For three decades, that has been a major focus of my hands-on work: listening to and working with leaders, their teams, and their organizations.

What I have come to believe is this: while leadership as a discipline is very, very important, the personal and interpersonal sides of leadership are every bit as important as the great leadership themes of vision, execution, strategy, and the like. For what actually happens is that no matter how great a vision or a strategy, the leader must get it all done with and through people. And there are ways that leaders lead that make vision and strategy work, and there are ways that leaders lead that get in the way or ultimately cause it all to not work very well.

Leaders can motivate or demotivate their people. They can propel them down a runway to great results, or confuse them so that they cannot clearly get from A to Z. They can bring a team or a group together to achieve shared, extraordinary goals, or they can cause division and fragmentation. They can create a culture that augments high performance, accountability, results, and thriving, or cause a culture to exist in which people become less than who they are or could be. And most of the time, these issues have little to do with the leader's business acumen at all . . . but more to do with how they lead people and build cultures.

It turns out, as neuroscience has shown us, that there are reasons for all of this. People's brains, hearts, minds, and souls are constructed to perform under certain conditions and dynamics, and when these are present, they produce and thrive. They think, behave, and perform to their capacities. When these conditions are violated or not provided, people cannot and do not bring visions and plans to fruition. And they all depend on the leader's style and behavior.

There are several aspects of a leader's behavior that make everything work, and one of those is his or her "boundaries." A boundary is a structure that determines what will exist and what will not. In the 1990s I co-authored a book called *Boundaries*, which laid out the principles of boundaries for people's personal lives, and millions of people have found the boundaries principles to be transformative in their personal lives. As I was working with CEOs and management teams, I began introducing those principles into how they led their people as well. The results were always profound for their business results, as no matter what role they played, whether a CEO, a VP, or a team or department leader, the leader sets the boundaries that will determine whether the vision and the people thrive or fail. The leaders determine what will exist and what will not.

Which brings us to the topic of this book, *Boundaries for Leaders*. While the concept of "boundaries" has been a familiar term in people's personal functioning, there is not much written on it in the field of leadership.

That is what this book is about. You will learn how seven leadership boundaries make everything else work and how they set the stage, tone, and climate for people's brains to perform. Literally. You will learn how to set boundaries that:

- Help people's brains work better
- Build the emotional climate that fuels performance
- Facilitate connections that boost people's functioning

- Facilitate thinking patterns that drive results
- Focus on what behaviors shape results
- Build high-performance teams that achieve desired results
- Help you lead yourself in a manner that drives and protects the vision.

And you will be reminded that, as a leader, ***you always get what you create and what you allow.*** So join me as we look at how to take charge and implement the powerful concepts great leaders use to create organizations, teams, and cultures that thrive and get incredible results.

BOUNDARIES
FOR
LEADERS

CHAPTER 1

THE PEOPLE ARE THE PLAN

My client, CEO of a $20 billion company, looked at me with one of those expressions that smart people get sometimes when something *extra* smart goes off in their heads, the kind of thought that captures even their own attention. Head tilted and eyes squinted, he said something profound: "You know what is weird?"

"What?" I asked.

"Everybody out there is always trying to figure out the right *plan*. They meet, they argue, they worry and they put all of their energy into trying to come up with the 'right' plan. But the truth is that there are *five* right plans. There are a *lot* of ways to get there. *The real problem is getting the people to do what it takes to make the plan work*. That is where you win or lose. It's always about the people."

He was right. Ultimately, leadership is about turning a vision into reality; it's about producing real results in the real world. And that is only done through people doing what it takes to make it happen. So, as a leader, how do you get that to happen? What are the things that *you* have to do to ensure *they* will do what will make it work—with a team, a direct report, or an entire organization? That is the focus of this book.

This book is about what leaders need to do in order for people to accomplish a vision.

WHEN THE "PEOPLE" SIDE OF THINGS DOESN'T WORK

This particular CEO had come to me for help with his team. They had become disconnected from one another, and their divide had begun to manifest itself in the rest of the organization. At the root of the problem was a breach between the leader of operations in the home office and the leader of the sales force out in the field. Communication had broken down, and results were slowing down too—all for no good reason, other than that the "people" side of things wasn't working. Even though the "plan" was good, the team was not functioning like a good team, with shared objectives and healthy relationships that would help make the plan work. Similarly, the culture was at risk, with negativity creeping in where positive energy should have been. The dilemma for the CEO was that even though he had a good "plan," as he said, and he had "really great people," they were just not working together.

As I meet with leaders and their companies, I find that more often than not, they have smart plans. They know their business, or they would not be where they are. They are strategic, talented, gifted, and experienced. Their "business" expertise got them to where they are, but as they rise to more significant positions of leadership, they need other skills in addition to what their business smarts can provide. They need to be able to lead people to get results.

What usually got them there was being good at the business, devising and executing "the plan." But now, as leaders, they also have to be good at something else: getting people to do what it takes to make the plan work. It is about leading the "right people," empowering them to find and do the "right things" in the "right ways" at the "right times." That is what will bring a plan to real results.

As one leader told me, "I wanted this position because I love the hunt, the strategy, the winning. I love focusing on how to make it work and getting there. But the longer I am at it, the more and more of my time is spent on the *people leadership* issues, and less on the work. I have great people, but getting them all on the same page and working together takes more time and energy than it seems like it should. Some days I feel more like a psychologist than a business leader."

How much time and energy it "should" take is debatable, but the key takeaway is this: the time and energy that you do invest in people issues should produce better results and create teams and a culture where momentum and energy thrive. And the work of building a great team should feel personally rewarding instead of draining. Put simply: the people side of it should not be what he was experiencing. It should be an investment with a high rate of return for you and for the business, not a constant drain on your personal and organizational resources. It should produce positive, not negative, energy.

As a leader, you probably spend a lot of time on the "people" side of business already—even more time when results are poor. You are always building teams and culture, leading direct reports, driving initiatives and change through your organization, and pushing for innovation, adaptation, and agility. And what you want is for all of that effort to produce results, and for people to be positively energized as they help drive the vision forward.

GREAT PLAN, GOOD PEOPLE, BUT POOR RESULTS

Sometimes even with all of that energy spent, results are negatively affected by the ways that different people function both in teams and as individuals. *Too often such "soft" issues become ingrained patterns that determine how the business itself looks and functions.* When added up, individual weaknesses and poor interpersonal dynamics can overshadow the strengths. All the smarts and skills of individual team members just don't produce the results you are looking for. Opportunities are lost, even as you spend more time and more energy trying to get people moving forward together in the right direction. Such a great plan, such good people, and still not getting the results you want.

See if you can identify with any of these issues:

- Results are less than the combined talent should be producing.
- Negative thinking and negative outlooks take root, and people sound like "victims" of the economy, the market, or someone else's actions.

- One or two people have too much power on a team or in a department, which allows dysfunction to seep into the rest of the team.
- Speed is absent as plans and decisions lag in a sea of desired but difficult-to-nail-down "consensus."
- The culture tolerates mediocrity or even poor performance.
- People and teams are not focused on what truly drives results.
- Pettiness and blame games replace healthy problem solving.
- Communication in teams and departments happens in "the meeting after the meeting," instead of face-to-face with all stakeholders present.
- Even though people have bosses and "performance reviews," accountability is not truly being exercised.
- Execution is not swift, and being "late" in launches or with other deliverables has become the norm.
- Celebration of "wins" is not as regular as it was, or as it should be.
- Morale is not where you need it to be.
- The business feels scattered and not on a focused, upward trajectory.

- Competing agendas abound and never quite come together.
- Some leaders and bosses in the organization build great teams and develop great people, but others don't, creating an organization that looks like a crazy quilt of inconsistency and uneven results.

Do any of these sound familiar? Don't worry: you are not alone. The frustrations described here happen frequently, even to very talented people and even in high-performance organizations. "People" issues tend to sneak up on even the best leaders, sometimes derailing even the best talent and the best-laid plans.

CHRIS: A GREAT PLAN HITS THE WALL

Consider the experience of one such leader: Chris founded his company by building on his success as a rainmaker. He had worked for a technology company and had consistently closed more sales than everyone around him. Like many successful people, Chris decided to do on his own what he had done for others. So, with some investors, he launched a new venture. "Why sell this stuff for someone else when I can do it for myself?" he reasoned. He was soon to find out the answer.

Things went well early on. Chris landed a few big accounts and built a company around those early successes. The new company grew quickly, landing more big accounts with global companies who wanted to use its equipment. Adding more and more employees,

Chris's company soon became a substantial entity, with revenue growing every year until it became a true market leader in its competitive space. The future looked good. Chris could see a public offering in the near future.

But within a few years things began to be not so good inside the walls of the company. Key employees who had joined Chris because of his high energy and can-do spirit began feeling overworked and increasingly stressed out because of what they called the "chaos." The company seemed to lack its original direction and momentum. For a time, success seemed to go hand in hand with the chaos, but slowly at first and then more rapidly, the chaos began to overshadow all that was good. That is when Chris's board, comprised of key investors, called me.

The board's concern came from what they were hearing directly from some members of Chris's executive team. The team told the board that they had reached the breaking point, that they couldn't take the chaos and dysfunction anymore, and that if the board did not do something soon, they were going to leave. That amount of talent threatening a mass exodus certainly got the board's attention.

In trying to get to the bottom of the problem, my first step was to set up interviews with all of the members of the executive team. I wanted to get a feel for what was happening. What struck me first was their love for Chris. They really admired him, the energy that he created, his passion for what they were doing, and his creativity about the technology they had developed. They wanted to be on his team and make what they had created succeed and grow. Even more important, they wanted to give their talents to the company, and they all wanted to be part of the endeavor for the long term.

But they had gotten to a bad place. When I interviewed them they were as dismayed and as frustrated as they had been motivated and inspired at the beginning of the company's journey. They reported feeling like they were running around in a thousand different directions. They would be headed down one path, only to suddenly get an e-mail from Chris about another new deal that required team members to marshal all of their resources around this latest, exciting opportunity—never mind last week's latest, exciting opportunity. Obviously this near-constant rejiggering of priorities created confusion and disruptions, leaving the rank and file unsure about whether what they were working on yesterday was still what they were supposed to be worrying about tomorrow morning. Or was the new emphasis the "main thing now"?

Even worse, Chris would send e-mails to his executive team's employees, putting those people into a state of confusion as to whom they were supposed to be answering to—the CEO or their own boss? Employees felt torn between two bosses and two agendas, and their own workloads. No matter how informal the work environment or how loose the chain of command, it is very difficult for most employees to tell a CEO, "I can't do that. I am busy." When employees went to their own bosses in frustration, their bosses would get upset and call Chris and say something along the lines of "We can't do this project 'all of a sudden' . . . and also do what we were already working on at the same time. And you have to go through us to get to our people. It's killing us."

Chris would not respond well, alternating between scolding them for not being "adaptive" enough and accusing them of stifling growth through negativity or by usurping his authority. Depending on individual personalities—some being confrontational and others preferring to avoid conflict—the executive team ended up either getting into nasty arguments with Chris or slinking back to their desks to complain behind his back. Watercooler meetings and rumors were rampant even though, on the surface, it appeared that everyone had fallen into line with Chris's latest pronouncements. In reality, there wasn't even one clear line to follow—more like three or four or more all headed in different directions.

On top of this, Chris had a bad habit of not being involved enough and failing to really lead his team and his people for good stretches of time, only to then swoop back in with what his team came to call intermittent "micro-downbursts." When the mood struck him, Chris would drop in uninvited on one of his executive's turf "just to help," but he would end up upsetting team members and demotivating the team's leader. Too often the team was already struggling with its own cohesion and thus wasn't able to block Chris's interference in a constructive manner. Everyone, it seemed, had begun to feel powerless to deal with Chris's leadership; they couldn't figure out how to get him to lead differently. And he was such a nice guy, to top it off.

In all of this, what struck me in my first interview with Chris was the extent to which *Chris* felt and sounded a bit like a victim. He was "busting his butt," as he put it, "for everyone" and feeling extremely unappreciated by the troops. "I am creating all of this opportunity for them and what do I get? Whining and complaining." *What he couldn't seem to understand was that they were feeling what they were feeling for good reasons.* He just didn't get it. But what also struck me was that *there were no "bad guys" anywhere in the mix*—only good and talented people, all trying to do the best they could.

The board's concerns about Chris's leadership skills had reached a critical moment. It had gotten to the point where the board of directors started talking with Chris about the possibility of a buyout that would send him packing. One board member confided to me: "I don't have a lot of hope for your being able to fix this. The only answers are to bring in a new CEO, or sell it." But without Chris's drive and skills at generating revenue, how would the board replace him without taking a big hit? At the same time, if a new CEO were brought in to assume the helm, then it was hard to imagine Chris, the founder of the company, wanting to stay. How could he possibly let go of his "baby"? At forty-four, it seemed like his entire life and his future were bound up in the company's success.

Both outcomes seemed completely unattractive, so . . . what to do? Obviously you could treat the symptoms—such as trying to get Chris to behave and stop doing more deals than they could deliver, or getting the rest of his team to communicate better. Or you could bring someone in to be a real leader and take charge of the operations in ways that Chris was not doing. Certainly all of those things would be really good ideas, but from my perspective the problem was deeper. If the company was ever going to realize its vision and make its revenue targets for the next year and beyond, a new path was needed.

What was the real issue?

THE NEED FOR BOUNDARIES

The issue was that Chris and his team had failed to establish the boundaries that would positively drive organizational health and the boundaries that would immunize them against sickness. The only solution was for the board to find a way to help Chris achieve his potential and for Chris to find a way to be the kind of leader his company needed. Over the course of the next eighteen months, I was able to work with Chris and his team, and they began to lead the company in a way that made it possible to leverage its many strengths . . . through the concepts that we will cover in this book.

The good news is that the issues Chris and his team faced—the issues that many of you face in your own organizations—are fixable. **When leaders lead in ways that people's brains can follow, good results follow as well.** No matter where you see yourself in this story, I want you to remember that when leaders begin to behave differently, most of the issues that hamper results and harm company culture are truly fixable. You can get the results you desire, if you lead in ways that people can actually follow.

You might be like Chris, a great performer, a master in working the "business and the plan," but now you find yourself hitting some hard realities about how to lead others to the same level of performance that you have achieved.

You might be like Chris's board of directors, the boss of someone whose performance you really need, even as you must find a way to help him transform his dysfunctional leadership style in a way that can bring results and make people thrive.

You might be on an executive team led by a dysfunctional leader who often makes it difficult for you and your team to succeed.

You might be further down in the organization, feeling the effects of dysfunctional leadership issues above you, and have a desire to make things better but don't know how to do that from your level.

Or you might be a spouse, family member, or a friend of someone for whom this scenario is all too familiar. You want to help them figure out what they could do to feel better about work and about themselves.

Wherever you might find yourself, remember that there are good reasons for the results you are not getting. And there are answers that work. But to get to the answers, you will have to get to a very important realization first.

CHAPTER 2

RIDICULOUSLY IN CHARGE

Recently I was discussing similar people issues with another CEO. I asked him why he thought those problems were there. He talked about some reasons, most of which had to do with the various players involved, and also the constellations of a few teams. But then I asked him a simple question.

"And why is that?" I asked.

"What do you mean? I think it is the reasons I just said."

"I know the reasons you said, but why do those reasons exist?" I continued.

"I don't get it. . . . What do you mean?" he asked further.

"Who is the leader? Who is in charge of the culture? Who is in charge of the ways that it is working, the fact that all of that exists?" I pushed.

He just looked at me, and nodded. "I am," he said.

"So what kind of culture would you *like*?" I asked. "What kind of culture would drive the business forward if you had it?"

When he thought about that, he looked upward, lost in thought for a moment. Then he got out of the "problem-speak" mode, and I could see a shift in his energy as a new vision of a different culture sprang to life in his eyes. He began to describe a company culture that was positive, highly energetic, accountable, innovative, and performance oriented. He came alive when he talked about it.

"So why don't you build *that* kind of culture?" I asked.

For a nanosecond it seemed like he was about to reflexively blurt out a reason why it could not happen, but then he paused and said something I will never forget:

"You know, when you think about it . . .
I *am* ridiculously in charge."

At that point, I knew he got it. He realized that he would have exactly the culture that he creates and would not have the one he did not allow to exist. Whatever culture he got, he was either building it or allowing it. He was "ridiculously in charge," that is, "*totally* in charge," and at that moment, he owned it. It was his. It was truly up to him. As a leader, he was going to get what he built, or what he allowed.

BOUNDARIES: WHAT YOU CREATE AND WHAT YOU ALLOW

What are boundaries? They are made up of two essential things: *what you create and what you allow.* A "boundary" is a property line. It defines where your property begins and ends. If you think about your home, on your property, you can define what is going to happen there, and what is not. You are "ridiculously in charge" of the vision, the people you invite in, what the goals and purposes are going to be, what behavior is going to be allowed and what isn't. You build and allow the culture. It is all yours. You set the agenda, and you make the rules. And what you find there, you own. It is your creation or your allowances that have made it be. Simply stated, the leaders' boundaries define and shape what is going to be and what isn't.

In the end, as a leader, you are always going to get a combination of two things: what you create and what you allow.

I was leading an offsite for a health care company recently about a range of leadership issues, and the director of HR asked a key question.

"So, how can you know if the problem is about the leader, or the follower?"

He went on to talk about "problem employees," who don't perform or who are difficult. "There is such a thing as a 'follower' who isn't getting it, right?" he said.

"Sure," I said. "But on *whose* watch? In *whose* culture? Who built the team that allows that? Who is over that employee that is a 'problem'? And who is over the employee that allows employees like that to be that way? And if that employee is confused about the strategy or direction, *who* is it that sets that strategy and direction for their team or the organization? In the language of Apple, 'who is the DRI, the directly responsible individual?'"

Who owns it?

It is a central principle of boundaries: **ownership**.

Ultimately, *leaders* own it. They are the ones who define and create the boundaries that drive the behavior that forms the identity of teams and culture and sets the standards of performance. Leaders define the direction and are responsible for making it happen. And they are responsible for the accountability systems that ensure that it does happen. *It always comes back to leadership and the boundaries they allow to exist on their property.* Leaders define the boundaries, and successful leaders define them well in several key areas:

- The vision, the focus, the attention, and the activities that create forward movement are defined by leaders.
- The emotional climate of the organization and its culture is created and sustained by leaders.
- The unity and connectedness of the organization and the teams are built or fragmented by leaders.
- The thinking and beliefs of the organization are sown and grown by leaders.
- The amount and kinds of control and empowerment that people have are given and required by leaders.
- The performance and development of their teams and direct reports are stewarded by leaders.
- The leadership of oneself, which entails establishing one's own boundaries and stewardship of the organization, is required by leaders.

Leaders, through a handful of essential boundaries, make sure certain things happen, prevent other things from happening, and keep it all moving forward. In the chapters that follow, I will show you how leaders establish intentional boundaries that create organizations where people's brains actually can work and bring about results. We will also see an important "negative" function of the leader's boundaries—that is, what a leader has to "not allow." What the leader has to say no to and how to prevent those things from existing in the organization. Leaders are a positive force for good and a negative force against bad. You know what they are for and what they are against.

Positively, they establish intentional structures, values, norms, practices, and disciplines that build what they desire. As we shall see, they figure out what should be attended to that will actually turn their vision into reality, and they keep their people, teams, and organizations focused on those things and away from distractions. They build the emotional climate that will motivate, empower, and unify their people. They act as guardians of the belief systems that distinguish the culture, making sure that it is optimistic and energizing. They help their people define what they have control over that will drive results and empower them to take action. They build healthy, well-aligned teams with values and behaviors to drive results.

Negatively, they set limits on confusion and distraction. They prohibit practices and behaviors that sow the seeds of a negative emotional climate in any way, realizing that toxic behavior and emotions impede high performance. They disallow silos, compartmentalization, individual agendas, fragmentation, isolation, or divisions among their people. In their push for empowerment and for people taking control and responsibility, they do not tolerate negativity, helplessness, powerlessness, or victimhood. They do not allow teams to develop dysfunctional patterns that keep them from moving forward, and they immunize their teams against failure. And they make sure that nothing exists in their culture that works against the vision and the drive for results, or against people being developed into all that they can be.

FOCUS AND ENERGY

But this positive and negative boundary-setting does not happen by itself. It takes energy and focus. As one founder of a very successful enterprise described it to me:

> *When I started my organization, no one told me that half of my energy would be spent actually building and leading it and the other half, or even more, would be spent protecting and defending it against all of the things other people wanted it to be. It takes a ferocious amount of spinal fortitude to not end up making a crappy mix of your vision and endless bits and scraps from others who didn't have the cojones to start something themselves.*

Well said. You don't want a "crappy mix" of your vision plus bits and scraps from others that don't quite fit. In fact, you don't have to settle for a random mix at all. Once you come to appreciate that you are truly "ridiculously in charge," you can establish and realize the vision that you have for your company, your team, your department, your project, or whatever else you lead. Whether you are the CEO or lead a small work team, you are ridiculously in charge if you are the leader. And you can certainly protect it and defend it against that which would infect it, derail it, or bring it down. You will get what you *create* and what you *allow*. Your boundaries will define and make that happen as you step up and set them.

You may be beginning to lead something new, or you may be focusing on turning something around and making it better. A leader's clear boundaries are often what an organization is waiting for, and when it happens, it can create the most valuable company in the world. When a leader steps up and leads, and sets boundaries that provide clarity that cuts through the noise, it is a new day.

For example, when Steve Jobs returned to Apple as CEO, the company was in trouble. After diagnosing the problem as a lack of focus and by pruning 70 percent of Apple's models and products, Jobs brought the company a much-needed moment of clarity through setting a ***positive*** boundary:

> *After a few weeks, Jobs finally had enough. "Stop!" he shouted at one big product strategy session. "This is crazy." He grabbed a Magic Marker, padded to a whiteboard, and drew a horizontal and vertical line to make a four-squared chart. "Here's what we need," he continued. Atop the two columns he wrote "Consumer" and "Pro"; he labeled the two rows "Desktop" and "Portable." Their job, he said, was to make four great products, one for each quadrant. "The room was in dumb silence," Schiller recalled.**

---

* Walter Isaacson, *Steve Jobs* (New York: Simon & Schuster, 2011).

In my view, the silence came from the profound clarity that such a positive boundary creates. From that point on, when it came to making computers, Apple employees knew what they were supposed to be working on as well as what they were *not* supposed to be working on. Jobs helped them "attend" to what was important, and "inhibited" everything else. He said that he was as proud of what Apple "didn't make" as he was of what they did make.

The very clear boundary Jobs set defined the purpose and the focus of all of Apple's efforts going forward. Through the act of setting such a boundary, Jobs gave his people the freedom to focus. They were no longer pulled in a thousand different directions—quite the opposite from the conditions Chris's actions had stimulated at his company.

Besides giving direction, good leadership boundaries also establish the norms and behaviors that drive success. They build unity and energy. They focus that energy and attention on what is important. They build optimism and empower people to do what they truly have the power to do to drive results. They set the conditions and standards for great teams and culture, as we shall see.

On the flip side, good leadership boundaries diminish bad behavior and forge an immune system that automatically identifies, isolates, and stamps out toxins, infections, or other viral patterns that would make the organization sick or lead it away from its values, mission, purpose, and results. Strong leaders set up the kind of culture and structures that will deal with negative behavior quickly and effectively so that it never takes root. If you truly build a high-performance culture, for example, it will not allow weak performance or nonperformance to take hold. Instead the culture responds by either fixing it or removing the source. All of that flows out of the boundaries established by the leader.

THE LEADER AND THE BRAIN

As neuroscientists have shown in recent years, the very best leadership skills are rooted in how people think, in how our brains are constructed and how they operate. Our brains, as we'll begin to explore in the next chapter, are designed to work in specific ways, in specific conditions, with specific requirements. When those conditions are met, smart and talented people flourish. They win.

On the other hand, when those conditions are not met, they flounder and do not perform up to their potential. It turns out that it really is all in your head—that is, your brain. It will not work well when leaders are doing things that inhibit brain functioning, or are leading teams and organizations in ways that literally make it impossible for people's brains to work to their full potential. In the pages that follow, we'll take a look at how and why we crave focused attention, positivity, unity, control, and other factors in order to excel. And we will look at why the work of leaders is always twofold: to make sure positive conditions exist and to rid organizations of the negative elements that stand in the way of high performance.

Just think of what is possible if the right conditions exist: innovation, creativity, problem solving, goal orientation, planning and organizing, initiation and perseverance, adaptation, self-regulation, and more. Think of what all that can bring to your bottom line if you tap into it.

As we look at how the boundaries a leader sets bring clarity, you will learn techniques and practices that will fill in some gaps, giving you clear leadership action steps to take. You will learn how to turn the tide that already exists. You will learn how to deal with the root causes of dysfunction and how to create immunity against these infectious agents. In doing so, you will also find new opportunities to grow and develop your leadership capacity while shining a light on some of the blind spots that may be preventing you from becoming a better version of yourself.

Sometimes the smartest and most talented leaders are very, very close to significant success, if they can get their "people issues" sorted out. I have seen them go from stuck and frustrated to focused and determined. And I have seen really great ones get even better. That's my wish for you: to help you figure out where strong boundaries could make things better, creating more results for you and for your mission. Working together through the pages of this book, I will share some of the mistakes I've seen highly talented leaders make. But I will also share examples I've seen when working with great leaders—leaders who understand what it means to be "ridiculously in charge" and who embrace that role and the power that comes with it; leaders who understand that boundaries can extend the possibilities for greatness across an entire organization, opening up the door of possibility to all.

I have seen these boundaries work in great organizations, from global companies with billions and billions in revenue to smaller private companies. The principles are universal. Whatever you lead, you can make it thrive. You are ridiculously in charge.

Let's get to it.

QUESTIONS TO ASK

As you focus on the "plan," how can you add focus to how you lead the people who have to execute the plan?

What kind of culture, team, or organization have you created or allowed?

How do you and your team need to be different from what you are?

How do you hold yourself and your team accountable for the results you are getting?

What does it mean for you to be "ridiculously" in charge?

CHAPTER 3

LEADING SO BRAINS CAN WORK

Remember the old saying "Come on, this is not brain surgery"? It was meant to convey the simplicity of an answer or a concept, and often meant to prod people to get off their butts and do what is obvious. That is how it is with a leader's boundaries. It is profoundly simple. You do not have to be a brain surgeon to establish the boundaries that are usually made by a great leader.

But at the same time, underneath it all, it really *is* brain surgery, because the reason that a leader's boundaries work is that they *actually make it possible for people's brains to function as they were designed.* Said another way, if you are trying to lead people and do not establish effective boundaries, your people will not be able to do what you need and want them to do because their brains can't work that way. You will build an organization full of geniuses who are producing brain-impaired results. "That explains a lot," as one executive said to me. "Those are the kinds of results I am getting from all these smart people I hired."

Why is that? Just like a computer, the brain operates according to certain processes that are *hardwired* or encoded in the system. Ignore the operating instructions, and the brain flounders. But as a leader, if you understand how the brain works and what will make it function optimally, you can create the right conditions to help your people be at their best, and when they're at their best, the organization thrives and positive results stream in. Show me a person, a team, or a company that gets results, and I will show you the leadership boundaries that make it possible.

But here's the catch: *if leadership is operating in a way that makes any of those brain functions unable to perform, or creates a team or culture in which they cannot work, results will be weakened and the vision damaged.* And that is exactly what we see in many cases. Leaders often construct teams and cultures that impede healthy human behaviors—all the while wondering why they do not get results "with all these smart people." You can be sure, for example, that Apple had plenty of smart people hanging around when they were not producing results. But confusion and lack of clarity hampered those brains from getting anything done.

So now, let's get specific. What are these brain processes that the leader's boundaries enable to work? Beginning in this chapter and in those that follow, we will take a look at several brain functions that are critical for high performance. Neuroscience has shown that when these processes are cultivated and protected—which is exactly what strong boundaries provide—good things happen. Let's start by looking at what brain scientists call the "executive functions" of the brain.

THE BRAIN'S EXECUTIVE FUNCTIONS

In brain terminology, executive functions are needed to achieve any kind of purposeful activity—such as reaching a goal, driving a vision forward, conquering an objective. Whether driving a car or making and selling cars, the brain relies on three essential processes:

Attention: the ability to focus on relevant stimuli, and block out what is not relevant: "Pay attention!"

Inhibition: the ability to "not do" certain actions that could be distracting, irrelevant, or even destructive: "Don't do that!"

Working Memory: the ability to retain and access relevant information for reasoning, decision making, and taking future actions: "Remember and build on *relevant* information."

In other words, our brains need to be able to: (a) focus on something specific, (b) not get off track by focusing on or being assaulted by other data inputs or toxicity, and (c) continuously be aware of relevant information at all times.

Take the example of driving a car to the grocery store. In order to complete the task, your brain has to rely on all three executive functions: attending, inhibiting, and remembering. It must:

Attend to Important Data: You have to know your speed, where the car in front of you is, what oncoming traffic there is, what lane you are in, which turn is next, etc.

Inhibit What Is Irrelevant or Destructive: You cannot drive if you are texting or trying to watch a video, or if someone in the passenger seat is screaming at you.

Use Working Memory: You can't just be put into a car, in a moment, by a time machine and know what to do next. You have to remember where you are in a flow. What was the last turn you made? How far have you been since then? What have you already passed?

Brain researchers say that "attention" is like a magic key that unlocks higher-order brain circuitry. When we pay attention to something, repeatedly, the necessary wiring is formed that makes it possible for us to learn new things, take the right actions, and achieve our goals. Research shows that driving that attention forward through repetition is critical to establishing new neural pathways and new connections—and thus new learning, growth, and insights. Attention is essential, but not enough. It can't really thrive without enlisting its siblings: inhibition and working memory. You need all three executive functions.

GREAT LEADERS SET BOUNDARIES FOR ATTENTION

In the context of leading a high-performance organization, it is much the same. Leadership must set the stage and ensure that:

a. What is important is always being attended to—attention.

b. What is not important or destructive is not allowed in—inhibited.

c. There is ongoing awareness of all the relevant pieces required to fulfill the task—working memory.

As a leader who is "ridiculously in charge," you have to establish boundaries that support and enhance the executive functions of your people. Think about these questions, which pertain to individuals, teams, and cultures:

> What structures, disciplines, and practices make sure that your people are attending to what is most important?
>
> What processes do you have in place that are inhibiting what is disruptive, irrelevant, or destructive?
>
> How do you keep people conscious of what they need to be conscious of in order to make it all work?
>
> How do you lead in a way that enables people to attend, inhibit, and remember?

Finding the right answers doesn't require brain surgery—it's not rocket science, either—but it also isn't as simple as a "to-do list" or "time management" or "better communication." As we shall see, you must lead in a way that ensures your own energy and your people's energy will be spent on what is important and on what drives results, while limiting and inhibiting distractions, intrusions, or toxins. In this way, executive functions serve as the leader's GPS. They are a tool for activating positive behaviors and emotions, for monitoring conditions and challenges, and for gathering relevant information that will be useful going forward.

Some leaders seem to come to this understanding more naturally than others. Consider, for instance, the contrast between two leaders of two different companies I worked with. Company A was doing exceedingly well; Company B was barely holding on.

Company A: Strong Focus and Boundaries

In Company A, the leader instituted one of my favorite practices, a simple routine that I have seen many leaders use successfully in dozens of different industries: the daily morning meeting. His philosophy with his employees was to "equip them, add value, and they will love it." So every morning he would gather all of the salespeople together for about twenty minutes and run through a fairly consistent routine.

First, he would name six or seven people who had some sort of victory the previous day or week, usually a sale that they had closed. He would pick one of them to tell the story of how it happened. "Tell us how you did it," he would say. He wanted not only to get to the "fabric," as he called it, of the key elements of the process and their behaviors but that the listeners should attend to what sorts of behaviors actually drive sales.

He would encourage his staff to ask questions of the person telling the story, as would he: "How did you get the lead? What obstacles did you encounter? How did you deal with those? How long did you wait before contacting them again? How did you close it? What did we do here from headquarters that helped or got in the way? Did you have to involve any of our partners?"

Next he would ask someone else on his team to share a helpful piece of information he had become aware of about the marketplace, the competition, or a product, or a segment that they were strategically going after. Or it could be a sales technique, or customer information, or something very relevant to their business in relation to their specific strategy and goals. His questions were intentionally designed to focus his staff on what was truly relevant, and also make relevant data clear and alive and in front of them each day—to keep it conscious in the minds of all of his staff. Said another way, he wanted to keep everyone's working memory, well, *working* on the right things. He was creating a flow.

Third, he would have people present a challenge that they were dealing with and ask the group to help them solve it. Everyone could pitch in ideas, share experiences with similar problems, and offer solutions. After no more than twenty minutes or so, he would end the meeting and send everyone to attack the day. The troops left the daily briefing engaged and performing well, year after year.

Company B: Weak Focus and No Boundaries

What about Company B? I had been asked to conduct a multiday offsite where we would diagnose and discuss why results were flat. They were a group of highly gifted people, very talented, yet feeling spread too thin—working harder and harder and yet not realizing their vision. Turnover was high, and morale was low. I gave the team an assignment I sometimes use to reveal how well their brain's executive functions were being engaged: I handed them all three-by-five cards and asked them to write down in as few words as possible what their strategy was and how they were going to execute it.

You guessed it: *in a room of eight people, I got seven different answers.* One expressed the strategy in terms of revenue goals, another in terms of target markets, another in terms of products and services, another in terms of market recognition, another in terms of profitability, and so on.

In practical terms, if you followed them out of the room and watched their activities, you would have seen one trying to run up the top line, another geographically focused, another driven by what she sells, another marketing focused, and one obsessed with the profit-and-loss statement. Certainly all of those were important factors to consider, but there was no cohesive "attending"—no clear focus—to give the group direction or an aligned strategy that people could work together to realize. It was as if they were working for seven different companies.

With this troubling information in hand, the team and I hammered down on getting agreement on what they should be focusing on so they could begin to execute *that* strategy—all at once, all together, all on the same page. They then drilled down to define more specifically what they were going to do and what they were *not* going to do to get there, and then the ways they would go about doing that. But here was the kicker and the big insight: as they began to get clarity, regaining hope and energy, *they also admitted that this process itself was new for them.* So I then asked them how often they got together as a group to focus on these kinds of issues.

It was a weird moment. Everyone looked at one another and no one said anything. Their silence told the story: not much. Perhaps never, I observed out loud. Finally, the VP of Research and

Development stepped forward: "That's not true; we did have that big strategy meeting out at Lakeview."

"When was that?" I asked.

"About two or three years ago."

Three years ago? Really? Compare that to the kind of daily focus and working memory meeting that Company A's leader conducted. In Company A, from sales to product development, to the lowest levels in the company—each employee could tell you what they were focusing on, why it was important, and how it contributed to the goals of the company. Executive functions were driving results.

Not More Meetings—Different *Meetings*

Despite the positive example of Company A, I continue to be amazed at how common Company B's ways of operating are. With complaints that they are already "too busy" with meetings, many leaders fail to make use of the very tools that will activate the brainpower and the energy of their teams. My hunch is that they have had too much experience with lousy meetings that disengaged and confused their brains. The last thing they want to do is have another meeting. And sadly, bad meetings are even worse than no meetings at all. So, make sure of this: *we are not talking about having more meetings.* We are talking about getting brains to work. Some meetings help do that and some hurt. But some way of getting people to attend, inhibit, and remember what they are doing is essential, even if it means changing the meetings you are already having, and having some different ones.

When those three needs of the brain are kept in the forefront of the leader's mind—attending, inhibiting, and working memory—meetings become something to look forward to rather than to dread, a time to renew energy, focus, and purpose. Good things tend to follow from good meetings in which the three executive functions are nurtured. Indeed research shows that there are tangible benefits when people are clear about where they are headed, energized to go there, and given the freedom to execute their gifts in that direction. People don't just show up—they soar. So, whenever you do meet, make sure it is clear what you want people to attend to in that meeting, what you want to inhibit, and what you are trying to keep in their working memory.

That's why I encouraged Company B to establish a regular time to get together with only one purpose allowed: monitoring and adjusting how the strategic plan was going. This regular time would help enhance executive functions: attending to what was important, inhibiting what was not, and keeping it in conscious awareness. Likewise, I encourage you once a month, for at least a moment, to pull out the flip charts from your last strategic planning session and ask yourselves together: "How are we doing in what we said we would be doing?"

It takes leadership discipline to put these boundaries into place. Company A had established a structure that made it possible for its sales team to optimize their executive functions. Through one simple boundary, the leader of Company A got his team attending to what was relevant in several ways: sharing tips and best practices, modeling healthy behaviors, and creating ongoing learning opportunities for the team. Every single day the team was reminded of what was important and was able to see their individual tasks and activities in relation to the goals and strategies that they had agreed upon as a group. It was kept right there in front of them.

At the same time, mostly without saying it, the leader was also helping them stop doing things that were not working or were not relevant. By sharing war stories and lessons learned about closing deals, their brains were learning how to separate the chaff from the wheat. The leader also created some explicit rules to inhibit or disallow counterproductive behaviors. For example, the meetings had two rules: first, "no whining," and second, "no problem solving unrelated to sales." These too created the right conditions, the right boundaries, that kept everyone focused on the right stuff. I have seen other leaders who set the tone by having rules like "no excuses, no blame, and no explanations."

WHEN BRAINS FUNCTION, EXECUTIVES FUNCTION

What I want you to see here is that this topic is not about meetings. While executive functions inform how we should conduct meetings, this way of thinking applies not only to meetings but also to interactions with direct reports, teams, culture, performance reviews, and almost every aspect of what a leader does to get an organization working. It means being a GPS that is always taking readings, always asking, "Are we paying attention to what is important, inhibiting the things that will not help or will hurt us, and keeping current?" This is why I chose two activities that are very different to illustrate leading by executive functions, so you can see that it is more than just a single "technique." Company A's example was with a morning sales meeting. Company B's was about reviewing a strategic plan. The point is that using the executive functions of attending, inhibiting, and working memory is a way of leading that permeates everything, so that the organization can make results-driven behavior as routine as driving the car to the grocery store. The organization's brains can work. It can attend, inhibit, and remember.

In other words, it is like this play on words: when a leader's *functioning as an executive* mirrors and ignites the *executive functions* of his people's brains, things get better—sometimes really fast. Not long ago, I was talking to a leader about this and he asked, "Do you mean how our executives function?" I laughed and said, "No, but yes. I am talking about how the brain works, but yes, it would be great if your executives functioned in the same way that people's brains do!" He laughed too. "Good idea," he said. "I like that."

ORGANIZATIONAL ADD

Sadly, many organizations seem to be suffering from the equivalent of attention deficit disorder (ADD). If you have ever seen a child with ADD, you have seen what happens when energy is exerted in the absence of focus and goal-oriented behavior. Many companies are like this as well. But for a company, "finishing your homework" means "getting the vision to have tangible results in a real world." It is doable, but requires the brain to work. As with the treatment of ADD in children, what's required of leaders is as simple (and as hard) as getting the brain of the organization to attend, inhibit, and remember.

The remedy for organizational ADD is found in the way that great leaders think and lead in everything they do. I was in a planning meeting in a company where I had just begun to talk to them about leading with executive functions in mind. The president, who had been very frustrated for about a year, began the meeting by saying, "Today we are going to be here for an hour and when we leave this meeting, we want to have answered this question . . . (and then she gave the question). That is it, no other topics." Then, when the group began to get distracted with extraneous issues and discussions that were not going to get them to an answer to that question, she brought it back. "Off topic for today. Back to getting to an answer." And they did it. More to the point, she and the team left the meeting invigorated and excited about the future. "We can turn this around! That felt so much different," she said. She was attending, inhibiting, and creating a flow of working memory. Others felt it too.

As I said, focusing on the executive functions of "attending, inhibiting, and remembering" is about literally everything. It is about how you see your teams, direct reports, and culture and also about how you use your own brain. For example, a lot of research has been done on the oft-admired "talent" called multitasking. Guess what? The research says that when we multitask, our brains run in a hampered state. Basically, multitasking reduces an astronaut's brain to that of a confused hamster. Try listening to two people at the same time, literally, and you will see what I mean. The brain craves "attention" in order to work. Neuroscience is proving that over and over. So, just as you need to attend to what is relevant and inhibit everything else, your organization does too. Lead in ways that can make that happen.

ONE BIG BRAIN

Here is a little more brain science for you. When those three processes of the brain are activated, results happen because they *enable the next level of the brain's executive capacities, which are the ones you really want to have activated in your organization.* It's the brain on steroids, so to speak. If executive functions of the brain are working well, and people are structured enough to focus, inhibit, and be conscious of what is important, they can execute the following list of behaviors, which actually are involved in producing results. (If you are a leader interested in results, and you think of all of your people doing these things well, this list should make you very, very excited):

> **Goal Selection**: They can choose goals based on priority, relevance, experience, and knowledge of current realities while also anticipating consequences and outcomes. **Key Words: Choose Goals and Anticipate Outcomes.**

> **Planning and Organization**: They can generate steps and a sequence of linear behaviors that will get them there, knowing what will be needed along the way, including resources, and create a strategy to pull it off. **Key Words: Generate Behaviors and Strategy.**

> **Initiation and Persistence**: they can begin and maintain goal-directed behavior despite intrusions, distractions, or changes in the demands of the task at hand. **Key Words: Begin and Maintain Behavior.**

Flexibility: They can exercise the ability to be adaptable, think strategically, and solve problems by creating solutions as things change around them, shifting attention and plans as needed. **Key Words: Adapt, Think, and Solve.**

Execution and Goal Attainment: They exhibit the ability to execute the plan within the limits of time and other constraints. **Key Words: Execute within Time.**

Self-regulation: They use self-observation to monitor performance, self-judgment to evaluate performance, and self-regulation to change in order to reach the goal. **Key Words: Monitor, Evaluate, Regulate.***

If you look at this list, it is not a leap to see your team or organization becoming one big brain, figuring out what is important, what is not, and getting it done through goals, plans, persistence, adaptability, flexibility, execution, and good self-management. Not to mention the innovation and creativity that follow. And the good news is that these are normal brain functions for humans. But it can only happen when leaders realize that they are "ridiculously in charge," and lead in such a way that the three executive functions are present. Almost every organization in the world has goals and plans. But only a select few organizations benefit from leadership that creates the environment and the practices that attend, inhibit, and remember, thus making high performance possible.

---

* Adapted from Gail J. Richard and Jill K. Fahy, *The Source for Development of Executive Functions* (East Moline, Ill.: LinguiSystems, Inc., 2005).

As we look further into the foundational role that leaders play in establishing boundaries, ask yourself these questions:

For Yourself: What do I do now to make sure that I am attending to what is most important? Have I defined it? What do I do to inhibit myself from getting pulled into what is not important? How do I keep what is important in front of me all the time? How do I create a "current river" of information, initiatives, and steps that keep what is important moving?

For Your Team: What structures and processes do I have in place to make sure my team is attending to what is crucial? Do they know what that is and are they aligned on it? In what areas is the team not inhibiting what should be inhibited, and what am I doing to eliminate toxins or distraction? How do I make sure the team is creating a flow of working memory with what they are trying to drive forward?

For Your Direct Reports: If I interviewed my direct reports, would they be able to say that I help them to attend to the things that drive the results that we have agreed on? Do I help keep distractions, conflicting goals, or destructive elements from interfering with their attention? Do I enhance or inhibit their ability to stay current on the important working memory?

For the Vision and Strategy: Is my vision and strategy clear and communicated in a way that allows everyone in my organization to attend, inhibit, and move toward it? Do they know what it is? Do they know what it isn't? Can they take steps in the right direction? Do they know what activities belong to the vision and strategy and which do not? Do they know how what they control directly contributes to that vision and strategy?

For the Culture: Am I proactively deciding what the key elements of my culture are going to be? Do those elements directly drive the attainment of the vision? Are there ways that I keep them front and center so that they are attended to? What elements am I determined will not exist in the culture and what is in place to inhibit those from occurring? What exists right now in the culture that either slows down or prevents the vision from happening?

You can see why leading in a way that helps individuals and teams engage their executive functions propels good results. They are paying attention. In the absence of this kind of leadership, you can have a virtually "brainless" organization, even while having great brains within it! An organization would be incapable of accomplishing its vision, as the *basic functions that the human brain needs to operate are not being supplied or supported by the leadership.*

In order for the brain to organize behavior toward new habits and new ways of performing, it must create new pathways to do that. In order for those new pathways to be created, people need experiences of being able to attend, be aware, and focus on their own thinking and what is going on that is relevant to their thinking. When you give them leadership that gets them to observe what they are doing, in light of what needs attention, inhibition, and remembering, lights begin to turn on. From those kinds of experiences come insight, which is like a lightning bolt that creates new wiring in the brain. But lightning bolts won't come if a leader is not setting clear boundaries of direction, both positive and negative ones, that define and support the paths for people to attend, inhibit, and remember. Clarity leads to attention and attention leads to results.

As a leadership coach, one of the questions I always ask myself is, "Does this leader lead in a way that is compatible with humans?" or some version of that. People are designed to function with energy and use their gifts and talents to work toward fruitful outcomes.

They do that from the moment they wake up in the morning until they lie down at night. From making the coffee to making computers, people have what it takes to get it done, if the right ingredients are present and the wrong ones are not. The leader's job is to lead in ways such that people can do what they are best at doing: using their gifts and their brains to get great results.

FROM TOP-DOWN TO TOP-NOTCH

I was talking to a very good leader, a longtime CEO, about the importance of executive functions, and he immediately bristled. "I see a big problem," he said.

"What is that?" I asked, wondering what could be wrong with attending to what is relevant, inhibiting what is not relevant and destructive, and being conscious of what you needed to know. What could be wrong with brains working at their very best? I was curious.

"I'll tell you. Because a leader who tells everyone what is 'right' to focus on can really be wrong about what that is. He might not know what he doesn't know. So I have a real problem with any kind of 'big-brain-top-down' focus. In fact, I hear a lot of talk about 'focus,' and I think that can keep people from innovating and seeing things they might not have seen before," he said.

I could not have agreed more, especially when leaders are telling their people what to think all of the time. *And that kind of leadership has nothing to do with executive functions or boundary setting.* Leadership is not dog training. It is the creation of the kinds of conditions in which people can bring their brains, gifts, hearts, talents, and energy to the realization of a vision. So, what my friend was afraid of—limiting innovation and discovery—is not what executive functions do. Not at all. In fact, they *support* creativity, because when people experience greater degrees of space for attending, they are better able to focus their attention. Have you ever tried to be creative while continually getting interrupted or having snowballs thrown at you? Have you ever tried to solve three different, complex problems at once? What happens? You lose your train of thought. You get overloaded with information. Your brain stops working. It bogs down and cannot create. When a leader provides an environment where people can focus on anything, including being creative, it in no way means that he is "dictating what to think, top down." He is just clearing the field so the game can get under way. They can then think it up.

Toxic, confusing distractions are different from the necessary "getting away from it all" distractions that are often required to reach "aha" moments—the epiphanies that can occur in the shower or while you are fishing or on a long walk. Those are good kinds of distraction, removing oneself from the task and letting attention have a rest. And even here, leaders can use boundaries to make creativity and innovation more likely and more routine through creating those spaces in a culture. Consider, for example, a company like Google, whose offices are filled with Ping-Pong tables and other *intentional* elements that encourage such moments. Diversions like these, which are planned and purposeful, can actually increase executive functions and creativity. As I told my friend, innovation and creation are an expression of executive functioning itself.

So, executive functioning does not at all mean "top-down" controlling leadership. It in no way means that the leader decides everything, dictates what reality is, or anything else close to that. In fact the best leaders will tell you that their strategy is always to surround themselves with people who are smarter than they are, and then empower them to do what they do best. And that takes focus in and of itself. That is not controlling; it is leading to set that agenda.

But just as much as leaders must focus on cultivating the executive functions of everyone else, they must also cultivate their own executive functions—what they are attending to, inhibiting, and keeping alive in working memory. As one CEO recently put it to me: "My biggest mistake of the last eight months is that it has taken me way too long to get the right COO in place. I have been *too distracted* [emphasis mine] by constantly putting out fires." Had this leader been using an executive function mind-set, he would have come to this realization and taken action much sooner. He would have attended, inhibited, and stayed current with that process until a COO was in place.

Good boundaries, both those that help us manage ourselves and lead others, always produce freedom, not control. It is the freedom to attend and produce. Freedom used responsibly produces results. It is a production cycle on steroids.

Top-down, controlling leadership creates other problems as well. Neuroscience shows that behavior changes and problem solving occurs when we are able to grapple with an issue, attend, and observe our own thinking about the issue, and come up with new insights. People change their behavior and thinking not because they are "told to be different" but when the conditions are present that *require and empower them to figure out what to do and to act on a plan.* Try giving teenagers a lot of advice and see if it changes behavior. They probably don't look at you and say, "Gee, Dad, or Mom, thanks for explaining reality to me. Now I will run out and do it." But if you provide context—by listening, sharing information and positive examples, setting expectations and consequences, creating a healthy emotional climate, and challenging them to do their best—they will figure it out and implement it. That is a lot better than just "telling them what to do." Chances are they know a lot more about their context than you do, and letting them figure it out is a huge opportunity to lay down more of the neural circuitry that leads to higher-order thinking.

Leadership is like that. You must not just give advice and "tell people what to do." You must create the environment, experiences, and opportunities where your best people can attend in order to innovate and think for themselves. As a result, their brains will do what they are designed to do: create new ways of doing things, and totally new things to do. And if you have the right people on board, they will exceed your wildest expectations. If they don't, you know what you need to attend to next: Find the ones who can and will.

TRANSFORMATIONAL MOMENTS

When leaders are leading in a way that helps their people and their organization attend to what needs attending to, inhibit what gets in the way or is destructive, and stay aware of what is relevant to the next step, the organization takes on a whole new identity. It becomes *powerful.*

This power is felt in a number of ways. First, it is the power of people being *engaged.* They are alive and focused. As we shall see later, they are operating in the "zone" of full engagement, using their best gifts in ways that are constantly stretching them. The energy of engagement is a positive force, and you can feel it in the teams and in the culture—from the front lobby to the corner office. When people show up, they show up. They "bring it."

Second, the power is a force for *driving results*. As stated earlier, the organization that is attending, inhibiting, and remembering the right things is in the fast lane toward making their vision a reality. Results follow this kind of focused energy, and the results create more energy that creates more results. Momentum turns into a driving force of its own as people know what to attend to and have control of those direct drivers of results.

Third, the power is felt in *constant adaptation and learning*. In the old world, where markets and economies were somewhat stable, you could win by having the best execution. Build a model based on a set of predictable factors and then execute to a plan. If you did that better than the competition, you won. But today there are too many things changing to win by good execution only. You have to learn and adapt to the changing environment all the time and then execute what you learned. So today, you take a step, execute well, and then learn from that step to know what the next one should be. Good execution is still essential; without it you won't know if the step was a good one or not. But, in a sea of change, you will have to learn from each step that is executed well and still make the proper changes and adaptations to the next one. The organization that is attentive, not distracted, and attuned to what is happening does that best.

Fourth, the power is felt in the *growth of the people*. In an organization that is attending, inhibiting, and remembering, people are forced to grow. There is a focus and there are clear standards of performance, with clear expectations that come from reality. But in organizations where no one is driving attention, inhibition, and remembering, *noncontributors can safely hide, drift along, and sometimes stay for years and add virtually nothing to the mission.* They become a drag on the organization.

Why? No one is really paying attention (attending). No one is telling them that their nonperformance is not allowed (inhibiting). And no one is really aware that they are not getting anywhere in relation to last month anyway (remembering), because a working memory is not being created. They are just looking busy, but not growing. When the executive functions are alive, people have to grow and perform just to keep up. Or someone will really notice.

Fifth, the power is felt in the *forward motion* that is created. An organization that is attending, inhibiting, and remembering is not standing still. Because of the learning, adaptation, and growth of the people, there is a strong forward motion. Think of Google or of Apple. You always have to watch them to see what is going to happen next. Take your eyes off of them and you will miss it. They have forward movement. Motion. Conversely, there are plenty of other companies that you could ignore for a year and you would not have missed anything. They are stagnant, even if they are busy; they are sitting still while the world rushes by. Executive functions create forward motion.

Finally, the *customers and the market* feel the power. Go into some companies, or fly on their airplanes, or shop in their stores, and you can feel the dimly lit energy of the whole organization. No one is attending, inhibiting, or seemingly remembering what matters. There is a dead feeling. But in a business where there are strong executive functions, you as a customer know it. You feel it. This place is on top of "it," whatever "it" is. And the "it" is exactly the thing that touches you the most, not only in meeting a practical need for their service or their product, but also, just as important, in your heart. They created a "transformational moment," resolving a need you had or giving you an unforgettable positive experience. They transformed whatever your need was into satisfaction. Whatever the case may be, the magic moment happened because they were attending, inhibiting, and remembering. And you as a customer could feel it.

Creating "transformational moments" is one of the most important things a company does for its customers. The moment when customers feel that a state of "need" is transformed into a state of "satisfaction," they have bonded to you. And creating those transformational moments requires attending, inhibiting, and remembering.

LEAD WITH ATTENTION, INHIBITION, AND WORKING MEMORY

Remember, never leave your brain at home. It is pretty important. But as a leader, don't lead in ways that suggest to your people that they might as well leave theirs at home too because they can't use them at work. You are depending on your people being able to use their brains. For that to happen, you have to lead in a way that enables them to **attend, inhibit**, and **remember**, on an ongoing basis. In the rest of the book, we will go beyond executive functions to address other key aspects of leadership and the brain that will help your vision become a reality. But for now, reflect on your leadership and ask yourself if you are helping your people to be able to attend, inhibit, and remember.

SO . . . HOW DO PEOPLE FEEL?

In this chapter, we have looked at three functions of the brain that lead to some other important things happening. We have said that if you help people to attend, inhibit, and remember, certain other brain functions will follow as well:

Goal Selection

Planning and Organizing

Initiation and Persistence

Flexibility

Execution and Goal Attainment

Self-regulation

This should be great news. It is what every leader wants to know, that is, that his people are moving things forward in this manner. And they will, as the brain's executive functions begin to work.

Unless . . . they feel so awful at work that their brains cannot execute those functions. Have you ever thought about how your people feel at work? You better. Because how they feel can determine just about everything, as we shall discuss in the next chapter.

QUESTIONS TO ASK

What are the ways that you ensure "attending" is happening in your team, direct reports, or company as a whole?

What are the ways that you ensure that distractions, or toxic elements, are inhibited?

What are the ways that you keep what is important alive and constantly remembered in a flow of progress?

CHAPTER 4

THE EMOTIONAL CLIMATE THAT MAKES BRAINS PERFORM

I was on a plane, seated next to a strategy consultant, and we were talking about the kinds of work we do. I told him more about the people side of my consulting and coaching work, and he shared the following true story.

The founder of a successful manufacturing company was in the process of succession planning and was grooming his son to take over the business. One day, as he walked through the factory, he saw his son angrily berating an employee in front of the person's coworkers. A lot of yelling, put-downs, and shaming—apparently it was an awful sight.

The father returned to his office and called his son to come see him. When his son arrived, he said the following:

"David," he began, "I wear two hats around here. I am the boss, *and* I am your father. Right now, I am going to put my boss hat on. *You're fired*. You are done here. I will not have that kind of behavior in my company and will not ever tolerate employees treated that way.

I have warned you about this kind of thing before, and you are still doing it. So, I have to let you go."

Then he said, "Now I am going to put on my father hat." After a moment's pause, he continued.

"Son, I heard you just lost your job. How can I help you?"

EMOTIONAL FIRESTORMS

There are so many great lessons in this story that I don't even know where to begin. But let me start with a question: What had been so bad about the son's behavior to cause his own father to fire him on the spot, leaving the company without a successor and creating some pretty unpleasant dealings around the dinner table at home that night? The answer: *the consequences of a leader making people feel crummy.*

In the same way that the brain cannot work without the executive functions in place, it also cannot work if it is drowning in stress hormones. The cold, hard scientific facts are that your people think better when they are not stressed, afraid, or depressed. Yet many leaders do not put a lot of thought into creating a *positive emotional climate* for their people, and sometimes they create the exact opposite. As a result of their leadership, they create stress, fear, and sometimes even depression.

The example of publicly scolding an employee is somewhat obvious and a bit extreme. You would probably never do that, but there might be lots of little things you're doing, none of them outrageous or dramatic, that still might be having a negative effect on your people. I'm talking about your "tone." The *way* something is said, apart from its content. If leaders speak in aggressive, angry, or "put-down" tones, if they use harsh words and overly critical ways, it can trigger a stress response in the other person. When that happens, the brain switches gears. There are a lot of ways this has been described by various brain researchers, but a common description is to say that it's like a switch going off from the upper brain to the lower brain.

LOWER BRAIN: FIGHT, FLIGHT, OR FREEZE

In the upper brain, higher cognitive capacities operate—such as logic, judgment, creativity, problem solving, advanced forms of thinking, working memory, planning, prioritization, big-picture thinking, empathy, and so on. All the good stuff that creates high performance—the things you want your people to do. This is where you would like to see your people's decisions coming from: their "higher" selves, the part that you pay to show up every day.

In the lower brain, there is not a lot of what we call "thinking" going on. It is only about "fight or flight." Mainly, two thoughts come out of that brain: "kill him" (fight) or "run for your life" (flight). More "action-oriented" than "thinking-oriented," the lower brain region is where instinctive behavior rules—the so-called fight-or-flight response. And when the options for "fight or flight" aren't available, it's as if a giant "freeze" button gets hit. We just shut down entirely. We get paralyzed. Fight, flight, or freeze are the only options when there is a high degree of stress, because the higher brain shuts down.

In the fight-or-flight syndrome, a collection of stress hormones are released into the brain, which essentially shuts down all of the functions that make us smart and, instead, activates another part of the brain designed just to respond to danger. Its mission is to stop thinking, and act.

In dangerous circumstances, it's a very good thing that we're prone to act first and think later. For instance, if you are on a train track and hear a loud horn blast, the last thing you want to do is *think*. "Hmm, I wonder how much that train weighs and what its velocity is? If I take the velocity times the distance between myself and the locomotive, and factor in how many bites I have left on my sandwich, I think I can figure out if I need to get out of the way now or if I have time to finish lunch." Fortunately, in the face of real danger, our brains do exactly what they were designed to do. Deal with it—either by fighting or by running away: ergo, fight or flight. No thinking, just action. Some refer to this as the reptilian brain; when it kicks in, we basically revert to having the intelligence of a lizard. But we get out of the way.

That should explain a lot of the behavior you have seen when someone feels threatened, no matter whether the danger is real or perceived. No doubt you've even experienced it yourself. People get defensive, they push back, or they avoid the conflict and move away. And, even worse, they may do impulsive things—speaking before thinking or acting out in anger.

TOXIC EMOTIONS

I remember one meeting I attended at a health care company when a guy felt put down by the CEO. The perceived threat immediately shifted his reptilian brain into high gear. He stood up, threw his notebook across the room, and stormed out of the room, uttering obscenities. He also left a multimillion-dollar compensation package behind, as the company couldn't figure out a way to let him keep his job after the outburst. Obviously he wasn't thinking in the higher regions of the brain—at least not until later, when he asked for his job back, only to be refused. Lizards, as you probably know, don't command high salaries nowadays.

But *the trigger for his response had been the CEO's ongoing harsh treatment of him.* It finally had taken its toll. The CEO was prone to stinging criticisms when he did not get the news that he wanted, or when things were not going well. His habitually negative tone had created an atmosphere of stress and impending danger that kept people on edge when he was around. You could feel it when you walked into the office on certain days. The mood was as tangible as a storm front.

It is easy to see the damaging effects of harshness when it triggers a reaction this extreme. But other negative triggers can be more subtle while producing even more negative and longer-lasting side effects. Sometimes the presence of a toxic culture reveals itself in the simplest of exchanges. One time I was leading an offsite when I asked a simple question about work flow. A VP started to talk about being a bit overloaded and then began to cry.

"I don't think I can take it much longer," she said. "He [the boss] creates so much work and he gets so negative when it is not done on his impossible timelines. I get anxious and afraid. I am losing sleep. . . . I obsess about it in the middle of the night, and work weekends and just don't know how long I can keep this up. I have to say, for the first time in six years of being here, I don't know how long I can stay."

"What are you talking about," her boss said. "I don't do that to you. I think you are a superstar and one of our best people. I don't get what you are talking about."

And that was the saddest part of this exchange. The boss was telling the truth. He just didn't get it—that *how* he communicated was even more important than *what* he said; that his unpredictable moods and his irritated tone and harsh words could put his direct reports into a threat situation where their brains would interpret his reactions as "danger." You can see "flight" ideation at work in the VP's comments as she said, "I don't know how long I can stay." Her brain was moving away, not getting more engaged.

"What no one knows is that there are times when I go to my office and it takes me a long time to just settle down after one of his moods," she said. "I feel like I lose so much time trying to get myself back together. And the other thing that he doesn't see is how much time I spend putting other people back together, too. They come to me and they talk about the pressure that they feel under. It is not good. And I don't even think he knows. But he has a huge effect on people, and it is not good."

And he was paying for it: slow responses, a dip in morale, high turnover, and a lot of defensive behavior otherwise known as "CYA." His tone had created the exact opposite of a high-performance, learning culture. As research suggests, people don't leave jobs—they leave bosses.

AVOID THE NEGATIVE, ACCENTUATE THE POSITIVE

Research confirms that how we view others, either positively or negatively, significantly affects goal-oriented behavior. For example, if we view someone positively, then we have a much greater tendency to pursue the goals that they are pursuing. So, as a leader, it really pays to make sure you establish a positive emotional connection to your people so that they are viewing you in a positive light. It's not enough to avoid toxic and negative connections; it's critical that you invest in building positive ones. Positive emotions have been shown to broaden people's range of thinking and responses, enabling them to become better problem solvers, more open to new inputs, and more efficient and productive. A positive emotional climate expands everyone's intellectual repertoire and abilities. This is not happy talk, but neuroscience.

Mood research in scientific studies has shown that moods and emotions, both positive and negative, are "contagious." We "pass on" good or bad feelings and "infect" others' well-being. One very successful CEO I know has put this research into a simple, powerful policy at his company: If any leader wakes up in a bad mood, he instructs them to "stay home. I don't want you bringing that into the office." As with the flu, it's best not to infect the whole office with your bad mood.

So, ask yourself: What kind of mood and energy am I fostering when I enter a room? When I give feedback? When I make a request? When I make a correction? When I communicate agendas and set performance targets? Further, what kinds of experiences am I building into my teams, reporting relationships, culture, and climate that make sure that there are positive chemicals flowing through the brains of my people?

Think of the brain as a bit like a car engine, where the chemicals and hormones in the brain are the gasoline that fuels the engine. Do you want to put premium gas in your car or will toxic sewer water do? The analogy is really accurate. One produces high performance, and the other causes a stall. Likewise, a toxic tone creates a performance downturn in the brain chemicals, whereas positive tones enhance performance. As the leader, you want to be fuel for your people, not seawater.

So how do you create positive emotional climates and avoid negative ones? Many of the boundaries and structures in this book will directly and indirectly help in that regard, beginning with paying attention to your own emotions and then developing a healthy emotional climate with your teams and in your culture.

GIVE BOUNDARIES, BUT CHECK YOUR TONE

There are two human drives. One is connection and the other is aggression. Aggression here does not mean anger. It means initiative and energy, used in the service of goals. Everything we do is either relational or goal directed—or, ideally, both. Basically, we are "lovers and workers." We have relationships and we do things. We connect and we accomplish tasks. Care and drive. Be and do. Love and work. The love requires a positive relational tone and the work requires drive, expectations, and discipline.

An integrated leader does both at the same time in a way where one affects the other. He provides a positive state of being and tone while aggressively accomplishing things with people. The problem in leadership is when we do *one without the other.* When we care about people but are not giving them the boundaries that lead to aggressive accomplishment—things like structure, goals, and measures of accountability—we fail them.

Lack of structure, a lack of clear boundaries, creates its own kind of stress. Think of a classroom full of kids with no supervision. It doesn't take very long for them to get out of hand, and to act out, often toward one another. But when a good teacher walks in and says, "OK, class, straighten up and get to work," they calm down and function a lot better. So the "caring, people-oriented leader" who has no boundaries creates as much stress as the tyrant, just of a different kind. When you let your people and teams flounder without clear expectations, you are not helping their emotional brains. That is why personal relationships where one person is "codependent" and does not set limits on bad behavior are so stressful, so full of chaos, or so destructive. Research shows that one of the key ingredients of successful group behavior is having "clear expectations" for the group.

But the opposite is also true. When leaders are only "task oriented," aggressively pursuing results with no focus on the emotional tone of their interactions, they set off stress reactions in others. People's brains freeze up. They don't work well when under stress. So the trick here is to give people the direction, structure, and accountability that drive good energy, but to do it in a way that does not create stress. And to do that, you have to watch your "tone." You can give feedback without engendering fear and stress.

Enhance Your Empathy

I worked with one company where the entire culture was being affected by the e-mail trails that came from the CEO. They were frequently of a "gotcha" nature, designed to let recipients know when they had not followed through on something, or pointing out problems in an accusatory tone. A significant breakthrough in the atmosphere and performance of the team occurred when I gave the CEO an assignment with two ingredients. First, for a while, I had him send his e-mails to me before he sent them to his staff, so I could check them for tone. Second, I had him ask himself: What would I feel like if I got that e-mail?

This little intervention had two functions. The first task was designed to build an "observing ego." What that means in lay language is that he did not naturally have the capacity to get out of himself and observe himself, in effect, to *evaluate* himself. He was just discharging his own frustration, kicking the can down the road toward others. When I began to evaluate him and fed this insight back, he gradually developed the ability to do that for himself. Before too long, team members were saying "I can see a change in him. He is calming down and not creating as much angst. The edge is going away."

The second part of this exercise was designed to enhance empathy. Empathy is the most basic human relational ability. It is the capacity to put oneself in the other person's shoes. When I asked this particular CEO to think about what it would feel like if he had been on the receiving end of one of those scathing e-mails, it forced him to get into the head of the recipient. When he did that, his natural compassion kicked in, and he said things like "that would not feel good. I would not like it."

OK . . . then don't do it. Don't blow up people's brains.

When he began to use these two internal checks before taking action—to observe himself and to empathize with others—his tone changed. His phrasing changed from "I asked you two weeks ago to do *x*, and I have gotten nothing. How do you expect this deal to close if you are not getting it done? Obviously you are not paying attention to the timelines. This is ridiculous. What is your problem?" to "Sarah, I need your help. We are behind on *x* and the deadline we discussed, and I need the estimates we talked about. Let me know if there is a problem I can help with to get this done. Drop in and talk to me if there is an obstacle or something you need from me to make it happen. But we really need it. Thanks." You might think that the impact would be minor, but you would be amazed by how such an elementary change can produce positive and widespread change.

Hard on the Issue, Soft on the Person

As a leader, you also have to worry about another problem. You have to pay attention to not only what's going on inside your own head but also what's going on in the heads of the people who work for you—what beliefs, experiences, and emotions live in their attics, so to speak—apart from how you behave. I'm talking about stuff in their heads that was already present before they even came to their current job. In psychological terms, this is called "transference," whereby people experience authority figures in the present as if they were authority figures from their personal pasts. For instance, if someone grew up with harsh criticism, shame, or nonempathic parents or teachers, those voices still live in that person's head and are easily activated by current events. As a leader, you may be thinking you are in an adult-to-adult conversation, but *simply because of your role, you are experienced by the other person as a parent figure.* Oops. So you might say something harmless, such as, "See if you could do that better next time." But what is heard is: "You idiot! Can't you do anything right? You deserve to be fired." You walk away from the interaction thinking you've given honest feedback while the other person walks away thinking you are a mean boss.

In reality, you shouldn't have to constantly worry about the noise in other people's heads, and later we will talk about how to deal with that issue in teams. But be aware of the fact that as a leader, *your position carries much more psychological and emotional weight than you know.* People want to please their leaders; they don't want to let you down. As a result, they can often hear criticism in ways that you never intended, and that adds to the complexity of your job as a leader. If someone is overly sensitive, then, sure, that's his problem and he must find a way to address it. But you can circumvent a lot of stress-induced bad behavior by not adding to the problem. *You can be steadfast and have clear expectations without being harsh, critical, or demeaning.* You can reset the terms of the interaction by watching your tone and by remembering the phrase: "hard on the issue, soft on the person."

And remember: The good thing about the extra weight that a

leader's voice carries is that even a modest dose of coaching and constructive feedback, delivered in a positive tone, can bring about great change in people.

THE RIGHT KIND OF PRESSURE

Ken Blanchard, author of *The One-Minute Manager*, refers to one particular style of leadership as "seagull management." He says there is a certain kind of leader who flies far away for a long time, then flies back in, flaps his wings and makes a lot of noise, craps all over everyone, and then flies away again. He leaves a big mess behind for everyone else to deal with. Blanchard is so right, and we all have seen it.

Unfortunately, I learned about seagull management the hard way. Years ago when I owned a psychiatric hospital business, I walked into our controller's office one day and asked for a report of some kind. She responded that she had not gotten it yet from the accounting department. I said, "No prob, I'll go down there and get it."

"No . . . I'll get it," she said quickly.

"No, no, no . . . don't even bother. It is no problem. I'll get it," I said, trying to do her a favor and save her a trip downstairs.

"No . . . I'll go," she reiterated, somewhat anxiously and a little bit mysteriously. I could tell that something else was behind her firm response.

"What is going on down there? Why don't you want me to go?" I said, wondering what secret she was trying to hide.

"OK, I'll tell you. If you go down there you will just upset everyone, and then I will have to spend the rest of the day dealing with it," she said.

"What? What the heck are you talking about?" I asked. "I never upset anybody!"

"Oh, yes, you do," she said. "You walk in and something isn't right and you get mad at somebody and then just leave. Afterward they are all afraid and in a mess."

"You have got to be kidding me," I said. "I don't get mad. Seriously?"

"Oh, yes, you do," she said. "We have a term for it."

"A *term* for it??" I asked. When something happens often enough that there's a term for it, it is not good news.

"Yes. We call it avoiding the 'wrath of Henry,'" she said.

I stared at her in disbelief. "Wrath of Henry???" I had no idea that I came across that way. Here I was, just trying to solve a problem, but apparently my tone suggested I was just focusing on what was wrong and not seeing the person on the other end of a problem. Needless to say, I felt awful and decided to go on a fact-finding mission. I needed to know how bad it was.

So I went and talked to everyone and simply told them that I had been made aware of this issue, and I wanted their feedback on how my approach had affected their work. Fortunately, the situation was not as widespread as I had first feared, nor as destructive as it had first sounded, but the truth was that it was a very real issue. I had a problem in that when I was focused on the task and it was not going well, I could get really bugged, and that came across harshly to others. I learned that people sometimes lived in fear of my coming into their work space. I literally had no clue that there was even the smallest perception of anything like that. I thought I was "Mr. Easy-on-everyone." Not so.

I had to do two things. First, I apologized, and second, I told my staff that if I ever sounded that way again, I needed them to let me know. There were really good results to all of this, but I never would have known it if my controller hadn't had the courage to tell me that I was creating a very destructive kind of fear.

THE RIGHT KIND OF FEAR

By destructive fear, I mean the kind of fear where people are *afraid of a person, instead of concerned with the issue*. The right kind of fear, or better yet—positive stress—is when we are concerned about some potential reality and the consequences of that reality, instead of fearing someone's anger, or shame, or a relational consequence of some sort for a mistake. Fearing reality instead of "badness." Positive stress is absolutely necessary to achieve results. Grounded in reality, it is produced when the emotional climate is supportive but honest and when the focus is on achieving a goal rather than on assigning blame or shame. Here is a way to think about this issue:

Reality is all that matters. The gap between where we are and where we want to be, which is the goal, does not go away by itself. We have to close that gap. And we have to deal with gaps that, sometimes, are difficult to face but motivating.

People need to be free of toxic relational stress in order to have their brains available to solve problems and look at the reality gaps that must be addressed.

Positive relational connections decrease stress and enhance brain functioning, and negative interactions increase stress and diminish the brain's ability to work.

So, do the math. *As long as my tone induced toxic fear in others, I was creating an environment that would ultimately take away from what I wanted us to achieve while adding to the problem that was bugging me.* Said another way, here I was increasing the gap I had been trying to close. I was making it harder for them to solve the problem. I would have been better off staying home that day, sitting on my hands, duct-taping my mouth—but no matter what—I should not have been trying to lead people with that attitude, making it worse.

Alternately, the "right kind of fear" *increases performance.* We will see how to do that in upcoming chapters, but for now, the quick way to think about healthy fear is that it motivates us to make reality better in some way, and to avoid bad outcomes. Here is how it works. If you are a procrastinator at all, when does your performance go up? Often, you come through just as a deadline approaches, which if not met, would result in some really undesirable outcome. For example, if you put off paying bills, when do you perform your absolute best at paying bills? On the last day that you can send it in and not get a penalty, or have the credit card canceled, or the lights go off. You become a stellar performer, 100 percent successful, because you fear reality. Similarly, I bet that if we plotted the "doing taxes" performance curve of the United States, it would go off the charts on April 14. Off the charts. Very, very, very high performance, and *high performance in a proven group of poor performers in that area.* (Think about that!) The reason for that high performance is that a healthy fear of consequences kicks in, in that if the forms don't get postmarked on April 15, there will be a price to pay in one form or another; the IRS may penalize you, garnish wages, or take you to court. So, fear of consequences can be good for performance, but it has to be the right kind of fear.

FEAR AS A POSITIVE MOTIVATOR

In business, fear can be a positive motivator too: fear of not making the numbers, fear of losing market share, fear of losing a customer or key account, fear of losing an investment if you do not perform, fear of losing one's job, or fear of losing the business itself. Love fear. It will save your life. Embrace it, look for it, and spread it around—but in a good way. It does not have to be toxic at all. It is just, said another way, basic awareness of the brutal facts of reality. These are what are called "reality consequences": "If I don't perform, I won't like the results." So, perform.

This kind of fear also adds to the good-stress performance curve. The way the curve works is that as stress goes up, performance goes up—*until a certain point*. If the stress gets too high, the curve goes the other way and performance diminishes. In other words, when the stakes are high, we get better—at least until the risks become too much to handle, and we freak out or shut down. This is why seasoned professional golfers, the ones with the highest skills and the most experience handling high-stakes events, tend to perform best in the U.S. Open or the Masters. For rookie players, the pressure is often just too great, and they "choke" just when they need to play their best. For the seasoned champion, on the other hand, the pressure brings out his best and he rises to the occasion—and wins. In golf or any other sport, you can probably name the clutch performers and the clutch chokers. If we could peer inside the chokers' heads, you can bet we'd hear a lot of negative chatter clogging the channels and creating stress that is causing the brain shutdown.

Reality consequences establish good boundaries that increase performance. They come in two categories: positive and negative, and both instill good and healthy fear. The negative ones motivate the brain to action, because you need to perform in order not to lose things like customers, investment, the job, or the company. When I was growing up in Mississippi, the plantation owners *really* performed in early fall to get the cotton and soybeans out of the fields before flooding rains destroyed a whole year's harvest, leaving millions of dollars stuck in the mud where no tractor could go. Negative consequences can drive good fear.

THE POWER OF POSITIVE CONSEQUENCES

But life is not all about avoiding negative consequences. There are positive reality consequences that increase performance as well—such as helping more customers, closing more deals, reaching transcendent goals, watching results rise, growing the company, increasing value, earning bonuses and promotion. Good stress pushes people to do great things, much greater than if there were no consequence to their actions. Just watch any winner of a sports event receive the trophy, and you will usually see several motivating forces (positive stressors) at work: the raising of the trophy as a symbol of the pride; the rewards and fulfillment of doing well; the tears that reveal the way the heart is overcome with humility, gratitude, and love; and the embrace of family and friends who made the dream a reality. These relational drivers can be even more powerful than traditional incentives.

Think, for instance, of what motivates a salesperson. You can be sure that the promise of a big commission drives his performance toward positive consequences. But you can also be sure that other factors are motivating that performance—things like the satisfaction of having mastered the skills of selling after years of effort, or the mental picture of his child graduating from college that the commission will pay for, or the high five he exchanges with his older brother or his father when he shares his success, or the sense of having contributed to a team effort in a way that is consistent with personal values. Put all of these factors together, and you get some strong positive consequences.

These two sets of reality consequences—the promise of positive outcomes and the fear of losing something of value—are among the most fundamental drivers of human performance. Use them together, and you have a formula for leading others toward great things. Talk both about the bad things that will happen if we don't get with it, and the good things that will happen if we do. "If we don't get this product out there, the competition is going to overtake our market share. But if we do, we are going to win over a lot of theirs. Let's go!" That is a lot better than yelling at people and making them feel "bad."

But remember that rewards and reality consequences also interact with other organizational and interpersonal dynamics, which we will explore in the rest of this book. Of course, if we were rats, then shocks and snacks would be all we need. But humans need more than that to give them the power and freedom to excel. Yet one thing is sure. A healthy sense of the positive realities that will come about, along with a healthy awareness of the losses we will incur if we don't perform, are good for getting things done. They are a lot more powerful than toxic fear.

PRESERVE RELATIONSHIPS AND GET RESULTS

As the person in charge of setting emotional boundaries, your job is twofold. First, do everything possible to create "good fear," the positive performance anxiety that activates healthy stress. The drive that says, "If I get with it, I can get something good and avoid something bad." Second, diminish destructive fear, which is communicated through tone, lack of structure, and the threat of relational consequences—anger, shame, guilt, and withdrawal of support. People need to know that you are going to be "for" them, even when they don't do well.

Think of it this way. What if your child thought that you would not love her if she made a mistake or did not perform to your expectations? What if when she made a mistake, you got angry, or gave her the silent treatment, or withheld love from her? What if she felt like there was no way to make you proud of her? And what if there were no structured expectations? What do you think that would do to her ability to learn? To thrive? To grow? And to perform? When we put it in that context, it becomes pretty obvious. Yet sometimes we overlook the power that positive relational security can have on performance, but it is there, and it matters.

A few years ago I watched an interview with a very young Olympic gold medal winner whose performance at the games had surpassed and surprised all of the coaches, experts, and commentators. When asked what she attributed her performance to that year, she noted that everything changed one day as a result of a conversation she'd had with her parents. They had noticed the stress that she was under and how at times she would get nervous to the degree that it was affecting her ability to do her best. They sat her down, she explained in the interview, and reminded her that *it was OK if she made a mistake, if she didn't win, or if she blew it*. Don't worry about it, they emphasized, and reminded her that they would love her just as much if she made a mistake, fell off the bar, or otherwise blew it. With uncharacteristic wisdom for someone so young, she went on to say that knowing that failing was OK made her able to succeed. She didn't have to worry about what her parents were going to think, and the security of that relationship *freed her up to just think about what she was doing, and to do what she was focused on doing*. In other words, *there were no relational consequences to making a mistake. They would not shame her, be angry, hate her, or withdraw support.* So she was free to use every mistake as a learning opportunity and free to do the best she could at any moment.

That is what people need from their leaders, the knowledge that their leader is *for their success,* and if a mistake is made, that leader will stand beside them and help them learn and improve, not punish them. Similarly, people need a culture in which leaders drive people to "get better," instead of driving them to be perfect or avoid making mistakes. Research shows that a "getting better" orientation goes much further than a "being perfect" orientation.

I cannot tell you how many times I have heard people say that their leader has his or her favorites, or once you get on her "bad side" there is no getting back. Watch for this tendency in your own style, and do everything possible to let your people know you will be supportive and for their success, even when they don't get it right. *This in no way means that you will be "easy" or allow ongoing patterns of incompetence or nonperformance.* That is equally destructive. You must always hold people accountable for performance. But even if the day comes when you have to let someone go, you will be like the father in the example at the beginning of this chapter. You will say something like, "So sorry that you just lost your job. How can I help you?"

ROOM TO GROW

Neuroscience has shown us that the negative threat that creates a fight-or-flight response is not good for performance. It deactivates the parts of the brain that we want to be awake and energizes the reptilian "threat" brain. In order for changes in behavior to occur, leaders must keep "fight-or-flight" stimuli to a minimum. Then they must add something else. That "something" is a combination of "attention" and "insight." The brain works best when it is able to "think about its thinking" and gain new "insights." Psychotherapists have known this in practice for decades, and now brain science is showing us why it works. They had always known that getting people to look at their own patterns, to observe them, and come up with insights was crucial to change and improvement.

We will come back to the topic of attention when we look at performance issues in teams. Meanwhile, the thing I want you to pay attention to now is how important your work is as a leader when it comes to laying down the practices that will help your people and your culture learn and grow. As research on mindfulness shows, we learn, grow, and form new behaviors when we are self-aware. The old term for this kind of attention is referred to as having an "observing ego." "Ego" means "I," and the observing ego is the "I" that looks at the "I." When we are able *to think about how we think, or think about how we think about doing something*—when we are truly able to notice and be self-aware—we are better able to move beyond old ways of operating and establish new habits and patterns.

That's why dog training, i.e., "correction," is no substitute for good leadership. And that's what makes us different from a German shepherd. *We can think about, attend to, our thinking and behavior.* The shepherd barks, and that is pretty much all he can do. So we just correct him. *But we bark and can become aware of our barking*, and thus be able to say, "Hmmm . . . I might do better if I did not bark at everyone all the time." We can become "aware."

I love German shepherds and have raised several of them. But I never had one of them come to me and say, "Hey, Henry, I was thinking about my behavior yesterday and I want to improve." But, as humans, we have that ability, to attend, to gain insight, and to change. But here is the key: ***the act of "paying attention" to what I need to do differently and better next time***

can't happen if I am afraid of what you might do to me now. When I am afraid, I am more focused on what I fear than on what I might do better. I want to fight or flee, or freeze. So that behooves the leader to build practices and times that make space for people to observe what they are doing and come up with ways of doing better, without the negative fear that shuts the brain down. People need safe spaces to observe.

Just like the boss and father in the beginning of this chapter, you as a leader must do away with negative stress in your organization. Observe it in yourself, in your teams, and in your culture. Build the positive boundaries that will drive "attending" to positive behavior and "inhibit" toxic fear. When toxic fear shows up, address it quickly and transform it. If you can get rid of all the toxic fear that shuts people's brains down, your people will become like champion golfers—total pros at delivering results when the stakes are highest.

QUESTIONS TO ASK

What kind of emotional tone do your team and culture have?

What creates that tone, either positive or negative, and what can you do to make it better?

How is your balance between creating positive relationships and high expectations?

What boundaries do you need to set on destructive fear?

What kinds of positive fear are you creating?

How can you create times, space, and an environment for safe observation and change?

CHAPTER 5

POWER THROUGH CONNECTION

It was the depth of winter, December 2008, and things were not good. The Labor Department had reported that more than 500,000 jobs were lost in November, a number not seen since 1974, and unemployment was rising. Investment banks had collapsed, the housing bubble had popped, and people in every corner of the world were worried about their future. As you might expect, Wall Street was not an especially happy place to work.

As a leadership consultant and CEO coach, I felt a bit like an ER doctor in the midst of an epidemic. There was so much pain out there and in so many different industries. It was an extraordinary time for leaders, not only because of the difficulties most industries were facing, but also because of the heroics and transcendent moments many leaders were responsible for. I saw it time and time again: good leaders rising to the challenges before them.

This particular morning I was meeting with one of those good leaders, the CEO of a division of one of the biggest Wall Street firms. He handed me a sheet of paper and said, "Take a look at this." It was a letter he had sent to clients describing measures his firm was taking to steady the ship. Intended to reassure clients, the letter detailed how the firm was going above and beyond what other firms were doing to help their clients. It was very sincere, as was the CEO.

But this particular copy of the letter was an ugly mess. One very unhappy client had taken a red pen to it, scrawling obscenities and accusations all over it before sending it back to the CEO. "You people should all go to prison," it said, along with other statements such as, "You are all thieves," etc.

"This is what our people are getting every day," he said, referring to the more than eight thousand brokers in his firm. "They are some of the best, most caring, client-oriented men and women in the industry, and yet many of their clients are blaming them for the market crash. It's understandable that people are upset, but the brokers didn't cause this situation. Yet they are the ones getting hammered every day. I know it is affecting them. . . . I can see it. Can you do anything?" he asked.

"Yes," I said, "I am sure I can. But I am also interested in that client, not just the brokers. The client has had his life flash before his eyes, and probably has lost a lot of his retirement money—maybe the college fund for his kids, and who knows what else. That is why he is so mad and not thinking very rationally either. Just look at the writing."

The CEO gave me a quizzical look.

"By taking time to understand both sides," I explained, "I could be in a better position to help the brokers help their clients and bring them back as allies sitting on the same side of the table."

He nodded. This CEO's strongest value was to serve clients in the best ways possible, and I knew we were on the same page. With all the negative press Wall Street was getting, it was heartening to see leaders like him who actually cared deeply for people. And he was not the only one by any measure.

We put together focus groups of the highest-performing financial advisers in about twenty cities across the United States. I flew to visit them and asked two simple questions: "What's it like for you?" and "What's it like for your clients?"

The conversations started slowly but picked up steam pretty quickly. Many admitted that they were experiencing significant symptoms of stress, including depression and anxiety. I remember one meeting where one man said, "I wake up every morning at 2:43." Immediately the guy sitting next to him said, "Mine is 3:47." Then a woman across the circle said, "I'm 4:15." Everyone laughed, and those three were really surprised to find that others were experiencing the same worried sleeplessness. Others shared different examples of how the stress was taking its toll. One man revealed that sometimes his wife would come into his study late at night and just turn off CNBC, which he'd been staring at in a zombielike state, not even realizing how long he had been sitting there. The groups I met with also talked about how their relationships were being affected, both personally and professionally. Some described times when they would be at the dinner table and their spouse or child would say, "Dad . . . Dad . . . hey, Dad . . . Earth to Dad . . ." until they snapped to it. Others talked about the amount of conflict they were experiencing at home as work difficulties mounted.

Even more unsettling to these groups—some of the highest performers in the industry—was how their work performance was being affected. They weren't just getting weaker results; their actual *functioning* was going down as a result of being in crisis for almost a year at this point. I don't mean just *results*, but *functioning itself.* I remember one man saying, "I have been in this industry for twenty-five years and have always been at the top. I have won every award this industry has. I have never had a problem with self-confidence. This is weird, but now I have trouble picking up the phone. I just sit there at times and stare at my computer screen. I have never felt like this. It's very strange."

The pain I heard expressed in these focus groups was greater than anyone had expected. But during those meetings, in city after city, something very powerful was beginning to happen within the group:

They were connecting.

Just getting together and sharing stories about how the down-turn was affecting them was changing them, and more to our point here, it was *changing their capacity for performance.* To be sure, they felt better and more supported and connected to their senior leaders. Likewise, they began to feel supported and connected to one another. *But I am talking about more than "feeling good." I am talking about the ways that their brains actually began to work again.*

"I thought I was the only one that had been affected like this," another man said, only to hear it reverberated around the room. Over the next several weeks, e-mails poured into the CEO's office expressing how powerful and productive those conversations had been and how connections made at the offsite were leading to still more connections now. One senior leader said, "I am amazed at the need that our people have to open up and talk about how this has affected them. They are very engaged as a result. They are getting back to work in a different way."

The initial connecting, in just sharing their stories and gaining support, was the first step in breaking the cycle. From there, I created a program for the CEO that continued to use the power of connection in teams to directly address the dynamics that were causing the stress and interruptions in performance. There were several components to the program designed to help the thinking and behavior changes that the downturn had created that were affecting both the group's well-being and their results. The damage of the external crisis had to be contained quickly, as it demanded even *higher* performance by these brokers, so we implemented a *team-based, connected* approach that helped them, in groups, realign their behaviors, thinking, client interactions, work structures, and so forth to the demands of the crisis.

The result was that in an out-of-control environment, the team was able to get back in control of themselves. The boundaries of these structures empowered them to contain the effects of the crisis. They began to think and communicate differently in their teams, and with clients. They discovered that there were many things they were still in control of that affected results, and they got re-energized.

I also urged the CEO to be intentional and systematic in creating even more opportunities for healthy exchanges among the brokers. They appreciated the chance to share technical insights with one another, but at this critical juncture, I reminded the CEO that *improving performance didn't hinge only on learning new technical skills or on working the right plan; it depended on changing the team's mood and improving relationships outside and inside work*. As one person wrote to the CEO, "I cannot tell you how helpful it has been that leadership has attended to our needs at such an individual level. I feel like this huge firm cares about my well-being." Another spouse of a manager wrote, "I don't know what you did in that program, but thank you for giving me my husband back." A year later, in fact, I was speaking in Chicago in a context unrelated to this company when a woman approached me and said, "I was in that program you did for our company last year and I just wanted to tell you it saved us. We connected in ways we never had before as a team. It changed everything."

In this crisis and in other leadership contexts, then, the question is "why?" Why does connection matter so much in human performance? And how can leaders create it and enhance it?

RELATIONSHIPS REDUCE STRESS

The first thing that connection does is mitigate the effects caused by the stressed-out, non-thinking lizard brain that we discussed in the last chapter. When we are emotionally and relationally connected to others, stress levels in the brain diminish. Put simply, *relationships change brain chemistry.*

One of my favorite studies was done years ago with monkeys, measuring the effects of relationship on cortisol levels in the brain. (Cortisol is a hormone associated with high levels of stress.) In this particular experiment, a monkey was put in a cage and exposed to a high level of psychological stress, including loud noises and flashing lights. They pretty much scared him to death. When the monkey was totally terrified, the scientists took a baseline measure of stress hormone levels in the monkey's brain as it was exposed to these stressors.

Next, the researchers introduced one change into the experiment: *they opened the door and put a buddy, another monkey, into the cage.* That was it. They exposed the monkeys to the same loud noises and flashing lights, and then took another measure of stress hormones. The result? The level of stress hormones in the brain had dropped in half. The lone monkey was only half as good at handling stress as the pair was together.

The reason is biochemical as well as psychological. We know that the brain runs on oxygen and glucose, for example, but it also runs on positive, supportive relationships. Other studies reinforce this finding. For instance, brain scans of children who lacked bonding experiences with their parents as infants show black spots where neural pathways should have formed. Said another way, their brains lacked certain hardwiring as a result of this early relational deprivation, and their ability to grow and learn suffered. More research findings about the positive effects of supportive connections continue to pour in, and they are equally compelling and conclusive: *our brains need positive relationship to grow and function well.* Whether for monkeys in a cage, financial wizards on Wall Street, or your own salespeople or team members, relationship is the key to high performance. Ask a Navy SEAL how important his buddy is.

So how do leaders create the boundaries and the structures in an organization that will attend to connection, inhibit disconnection, and supply the working memory to keep those connections growing?

LEADERS FOSTER CONNECTION AND UNITY

The first element necessary for unity and connection to occur is simple but profoundly missing in many leadership scenarios: the right kinds and the right amounts of time together. I want you to ask yourself how much time you are making for unity to be created with the organization, the team, and your direct reports. Both quality and quantity matter. *You cannot grow a plant by dipping it into the dirt once a year. It takes an ongoing connection to build a root system.* Obviously, the larger the groups, the more difficult it is to get the balance right, but it can be done. The best companies do not forsake the time and the effort it takes to get everyone together, even if it means convening town hall meetings, webcasts, and conference calls that enable leaders to address challenges and strategies. One company I worked with was on the verge of a huge split when the CEO saved it by doing a listening tour with small town hall meetings throughout the country. He got everyone connected, processing what was going on.

While some executives need to have their eyes opened to the importance of connection, others intuitively understand how to form and encourage these connections. One of my business associates bought a national real estate company, which at the time was losing over $100 million a year. He bought it anyway, convinced that its losses *were not business related*. The "plan," as we stated earlier, was not the problem. The business model was sound. But the reason it was losing money, as he diagnosed it, was "leadership." He insisted that if the business had better leadership and culture, it would do very well.

The very first thing he did was to establish an internal leadership university, and *bring all the leaders together into one building.* As he told me, "One of the biggest problems was that there was no sense of unity or togetherness, and it added to everything bad. They were fragmented. I had to get them formed as a team, with a sense of connection and oneness before anything else. And a part of that was making sure that they were physically together."

Three years later, after a successful turnaround, he sold the company for $650 million, debt free. No doubt they had better execution on "the plan," but the execution could not have taken place unless the toxicity, silos, and compartmentalization that had previously paralyzed the venture had been eradicated. It took leadership to get them connected and become "one brain," firing on all cylinders, with the energy that connection fuels. They had to get together, literally and figuratively.

At the other end of the spectrum, I once coached two members of a business partnership where, given the nature of their heavy workloads as their firm grew, they had less and less time together. As a result, they had each set up their own teams and systems, essentially creating two separate organizations. As sometimes happens in my line of work, I was called in "right before the lawyers"—that is, just when the partnership was about to break down for good. One of the first things I observed was the vacuum created by the lack of quality, connected time the pair spent together. As we know, nature abhors a vacuum, and so in place of feelings of unity and connection, feelings of suspicion and paranoia had crept in and were now causing all sorts of problems. Motives were questioned, behavior was falsely interpreted, and passive-aggressive behavior ran amok across the organization.

One of the suggestions I made was to encourage the two leaders to reconnect by attending to the "helping roles" they could play for each other, just as they had done in the beginning of their partnership, which had, ironically, grown out of a personal friendship, not a business arrangement. I also encouraged them to spend structured time together, including twice-a-week phone calls, just to catch up on the latest happenings with the business and with their relationship. As these connections increased and deepened, stress and suspicion dissipated. Fortunately, they were able to turn their relationship around, align around their company's growth goals, and then position the firm for sale to a larger company.

It makes you wonder whether the Beatles should have stuck it out.

USE REGULAR MEETINGS TO CONNECT

The last thing I advocate for is more meetings. Most leaders are "meeting'ed to death." But, unfortunately, most of these meetings are not doing much to build connection and unity. The answer is usually not *more* but *different* meetings of a certain type and more connection as a result of whatever meetings do occur. One of my favorite coaching practices is the quarterly offsite, which not only has a strong business agenda, but is also designed to examine the workings of the team itself (see chapter 8, "High-Performance Teams"). *Just getting together does not bring unity, as bad meetings have shown us all.* But neither does *not* getting together. For deep connections to take hold, certain ingredients have to be present that address those three executive functions I mentioned before: attention to things that connect us, inhibition of things that cause us to disengage, and repetition of processes that keep working memory alive. In addition, it also takes some focused time working on team operating values, with the team observing how they work together (team observing ego) and making changes that will drive alignment, relatedness, and results. This kind of offsite can pay huge dividends, financially and in other ways as well.

I'm not talking about Outward Bound–style adventures, trust falls, or ropes courses. I'm talking about increasing the team's self-awareness and about actually building the team's identity and cohesion through talking about how you work together—by discussing everything from behaviors to values to roles and responsibilities to decision rights to governance and more. It helps to set aside specific time for these kinds of conversations. Often with teams I work with, we do it quarterly as a structured discipline. CEOs and other executives tell me that just having that structured practice pays back the time and investment in big multiples. Over and over again, I have heard them say, "We could not have had that big win we just had if we had not been forming the team through those structured offsites." It takes focus to build high-functioning teams, like building any other winning team.

But it is not only the special times like going on offsites. It also helps to use some portion of *regular* meetings to check in: How did we do today on working together? Did we do what we said we were going to do? Did we live out our team operating values? I like the teams that I work with to just take five or ten minutes at the end of every regular meeting to observe their functioning by asking themselves those simple questions. Sometimes what happens is they might say, "Well, not exactly. There was one thing we kind of avoided because of the disagreement we have, and we really need to talk about it." Then they fix it, as a result of the "check-in" (see "Put In an Observing Structure" in chapter 9, "Trust Makes Teams Able to Perform").

The Right "Dosage" of Meetings

So ask yourself: Do I have *structured* times where my people know we are getting together in a way that creates connectedness? Are these meetings purposefully designed to give them a chance to be truly connected? To accomplish this, you must think about dosage: both the amount of medicine and the time intervals when you take it. Ask: How much getting together do we need? And what is the right time interval before you need to do it again? If you wait too long, you lose what was gained in the last connection and you are not building on it. For these kinds of meetings, continuity is essential. Similarly, if there are too many and they are too frequent, they lose their power, because people have not had time to metabolize and utilize what they worked on last time.

Then there are the regular meetings of just "doing the business" that connect you, or disconnect you, day by day, week by week, and month by month. The challenge of these meetings is that it's easy for them to lose focus on the important task of keeping those connections alive and growing.

Leadership author Patrick Lencioni gives a good example of a model of "meeting dosage" in his book *Death by Meeting* (Jossey-Bass, 2004). He distinguishes between four different structures of meetings:

Daily Check-in: 5 to 10 minutes

Weekly Tactical: 45 to 90 minutes

Monthly Strategic: 2 to 4 hours

Quarterly Off-site Review: 1 to 2 days

I have seen this kind of structure work well in my own consulting practice. But whether you follow this model exactly is less important than that *there is a structure, with attention to structure and dosage.* When you get these right, you will have *set the agenda around the activities that will drive connection, instead of just "getting together."* You are not overwhelming people with too many meetings, but you are having enough structured time together to drive connection. And what you are doing in those meetings is more than just getting together and reporting in. You are getting to real connectedness.

For example, in the work I did with the Wall Street firm mentioned above, I specifically structured an activity to allow brokers to tell me what it had been like for them in the previous eight months—emotionally, relationally, and in terms of their performance. I structured these meetings so that some vulnerability and sharing around the work could happen. Creating a climate that allows for vulnerability and high levels of trust builds connection. For connection to take place, people have to get real with one another. And that assumes that you have done the work to build trust. These kinds of meetings also get them in the mode of feeling safe, not fearful or defensive. As a result, you will see them less fearful and defensive with each other in the day-to-day challenges (see chapter 9, "Trust Makes Teams Able to Perform"). Another example: in the daily meeting that I referred to in chapter 2, the leader structured his daily check-ins to get people to share a challenge or an obstacle that they needed help with. That also got them into the mode of needing one another, helping each other, and thus building stronger connections.

THE INGREDIENTS FOR CONNECTION AND UNITY

So creating connections is another form of boundary setting. You are setting a positive boundary, or structure, to form unity. And you are setting a very firm boundary against disconnection and fragmentation. (Remember, you get what you *create, as well as what you allow. So create connection and do not allow disconnectedness.*) If you are a CEO, you have to be able to knit together a large number of constituents, or stakeholders, into a unified whole. Structure and dosage dictate why and when you are going to take the medicine, so to speak, but you also need to make sure you are dispensing the right stuff. We know from neuroscience that certain *kinds* of relational and emotional interactions build connection and unity based on patterns of the brain's functioning.

Here are some of those ingredients that build connected unity:

Shared Purpose: Unity grows when people come together around a shared purpose or goal. This can be the overarching mission of the company or a team, or it can be the specific mission of that time of getting together. Even in a team meeting, having a specific objective or a shared problem statement or an agenda will bind people together. That won't happen if purpose is not clearly defined and shared (see chapter 9, "Trust Makes Teams Able to Perform").

Awareness: Unity and connection grow as mutual awareness grows. I can't count the number of times I have heard members of a team say, "No one is talking about the real issues that we need to talk about." Many organizations suffer from "compartmentalized awareness," which by definition brings fragmentation. To connect with you, I need to be aware of you and what you are dealing with, and you with me. And we need to know and experience together what we are going through. And, really important, *we both need to know and operate from the same set of facts and realities.* Make sure that you set the stage in your team and in the larger entity so that people are aware of what is happening with one another and with the organization. When people feel like they are out of the loop, the seeds of disconnection are sown. And don't allow big problems to become elephants in the room. Bring them to mutual awareness. Name the elephant.

Nonverbal Cues: If as a leader you are truly listening to your team, and truly tuning in, the level of connection of the team will be markedly better than if you're saying one thing while your body language or facial expression says another. That doesn't mean you have to sit like a stone, but it does require active listening and engagement of both body and brain. Use nonverbals to show that you are open, positive, and warm. When you have to deliver hard news, be respectful but firm. And put your smartphone in your pocket, purse, or bag. If you are not an ER doc or in a crisis, it can wait. Some of the best leaders I know have a "no cell phone or e-mail during this meeting" rule.

Collaboration: Here I mean more than just asking people to give status reports, which are often best delivered by e-mail. Most of those meetings are snoozers. If you are going to meet, by definition that means that you need to be *present*—not just in the same room together—in order for connections to be built. Project updates don't require meetings, but collaboration does. I'm talking about creating a climate where problems and issues get shared and solved through the team's engagement with one another. Visions, ideas, and plans get birthed as the brains come together to actually do work together, not just inform each other. And hearts get connected as passion, vulnerability, challenges, and breakthroughs are shared.

Coherent and Relevant Narrative: We know from cognitive science that the human brain likes to organize experiences into a story, a narrative about who we are, where we have been, and where we are going. The more you attend to keeping the relevant narrative alive, the more connections you will create. In a company, the historical narrative is always important, but so is the current narrative about a new project or a problem at hand. Make a place for people to see where they are in the story, what it means for them, and what role they can play in moving the story forward.

Take, for example, an offsite I once conducted in the middle of a CEO transition. In this particular case, there was a deep division within the team about the company's strategic direction—whether it should migrate away from its legacy strategy as a big box retailer to something entirely different. Caught in the middle of these two worldviews, the team had become polarized, with one side hanging on to the tried-and-true strategy and the other mounting the charge in a different direction.

The two sides were able to come together only when I asked them to tell their versions of the company's story, beginning with chapter one of the old business, working up to the present, and then projecting into the future. As they did, I drew it in storyboard fashion on a big whiteboard for all of them to see. When they got together producing the story, they were able to see the drama and plot points in the company's narrative, and they realized two things: first, how they had gotten to where they were now (seeing that it all made sense), and second, that it was up to them to write the next part of the story. Now, with the insight that they were "in between" plot points, they were able to work together to develop an "in between" strategy for the short-term challenges they faced. Until they had a *shared narrative* for where they were in the near term, they weren't able to come together to plan for the long term. They could see in the story that there was a chapter still needing to be written to get them from the past to the future. *That became the short-term strategic plan around which they could all agree.* Unity came from adding up a lot of individual stories to create a whole story. Story, narrative, is integrative.

Conflict Resolution: It would be nice if business, and life, were all happy talk. But it isn't. It is hard, and it sometimes brings about situations where people feel pain, fear, grief, or anger. But avoidance of the tough issues, what psychologists call conflict-aversion, only makes things worse. So to create unity, sometimes we have to get right into the hard stuff, the things that people are really upset about. At some point every high-functioning team I have ever worked with has had to grapple with some very emotional and conflict-laden interactions *before* they get to their highest levels of collaboration and achievement. It is a necessary valley to go through before reaching the mountaintop. On the other side of the conflict lies a lot of good stuff—if people can hang in there. (This is why sometimes facilitators are helpful and many times, even *necessary*.) When people can go into the hard stuff and begin to talk about what they are experiencing, the power of relationships to transform those states of fear into courage, or anger into resolution, is a truly wonderful thing to see—something that no number of happy-talk slogans can compete with.

Emotional Regulation: At some time or other, we all experience very difficult, even destructive, emotional states. Fortunately we don't have to remain there. Connecting with others can provide a form of self-regulation. It can calm us down, it can help us contain strong emotional reactions, and it can transform those emotions into more productive, positive emotional states. We need others to tell us to take a chill pill every now and then. Think of the monkey and his new buddy. Or think of a time when you saw someone getting close to blowing up, or giving up, and her team was able to intervene to contain that state and even transform it. They step in and help one another. Or think of the opposite, all-too-common circumstance, where a team failed to provide that support because there was not enough connection.

I remember one offsite where the team had great conflict, and they were not helping one another with the emotions at all. At the height of the conflict, the chairman of the company closed his notebook and said, "I am done here"—meaning, he was going to quit. Everyone was shocked as he started for the door. I got up, ran to the door, and sat down on the floor, blocking the door. I said, "You can leave, but if you do, you will have set into motion a chain of events that will hurt a lot of people. Tens of thousands. Sit down for a moment. Don't walk out that door." He looked at me strangely as I was sitting on the floor in front of him. He seemed to be thinking, "Is this really happening? Is this nut really sitting on the floor, blocking the door?"

And then, still looking kind of quizzical, he sat down with me.

I then asked him what was going on with him in the last few minutes. As he began to talk, his eyes watered, and I could tell he was on the verge of tears. He expressed his frustration with the CEO, feeling like he continually "hit a brick wall with the CEO." He showed a lot of courage and vulnerability as he talked. I looked at the CEO across the room and asked him to come over. The rest of the room was on pins and needles as he did. I asked him to sit down also and then asked him what he was thinking. He looked at the chairman and said, "I am so sorry. I had no idea that I was making it this hard for you. Please, please forgive me." The chairman looked up, and for the first time in a long time I saw hope in his eyes. We continued talking, the team joined in, and there was a breakthrough that literally saved the company from a breakup. Tens of thousands of people's lives would have been affected if this team had not come together and transformed those emotions into something powerful and positive.

Emotional Reflection: Reflection is not problem solving, planning, or initiating something new. It is not judging. It is simply looking at things together and examining one's thoughts, observations, and feelings. It is "observation," as we have discussed. With a focus on the "here and now," it happens when people feel safe and able to express their vulnerability in the moment. It creates group mindfulness that leads to further insight and openness, which in turn breeds greater connection.

I remember one meeting where an executive team was asked to preview a CEO's company-wide memo together and share their thoughts about it. One person said, "When I read this, I just wish I worked somewhere else." I asked the CEO what he thought as he heard that and he said, "Makes me wish I had never written it. I can see it now." The team wasn't judging him, in this instance, but reflecting on the feelings the memo generated. Doing so helped the CEO build more self-awareness and reflect on the power of his words and his actions more deeply. With these new insights in mind, he revised the memo and was able to achieve his goal without putting the company or the team's unity at risk. But even bigger, he was learning to reflect.

Emotional Repair: Repair is one of the most important things that happens in good relationships. The truth of the matter is that we do have conflict, misunderstandings, reactions, and the like. We do get disconnected and miss each other. That is normal. But in good relationships, where the connections are deep and trusting, long-lasting damage doesn't have to be a side effect of honesty and conflict. Misunderstandings are short-term, feelings aren't hurt, and even when the situation needs to get fixed, apologies, humility, and humor come swiftly and easily. Seek repair and, when necessary, even have your team discuss how they would like to repair.

Listening: Probably the most important connection builder is simple, but aggressive (active and intentional), listening. It is simple because it gets to the most basic need in life. People want to be known and understood. You cannot lead them to another place if they do not feel like you understand the place that they are in. Leaders are notorious for not listening. They are often persuaders by nature, and in their interactions they try to convince people to accept their version of reality or their answers without really appreciating where the other person is coming from. They are guilty of "giving an answer before they understand." People's deepest need is to be known and understood before they can join someone or be led by them. They want to know that you "get it." Bill Clinton got elected president, in part, by doing exactly that. He toured the country, listening to people tell him what they were experiencing, and he just simply said, "I feel your pain." And they followed him.

Before you try to move people to your position, make sure they feel that you understand where they are coming from, what they are feeling, and what they are dealing with. If they do not feel that you understand their reality, your smart answer is not going to have any validity with them. Understand first. Listening is the glue that makes all of the rest of this work. Like the one I mentioned above, I have worked with several companies going through crises that were dividing the organization. Often I have the CEO go on a listening tour and put together day-long sessions, like town halls, to just listen to people and their concerns. Doing that and doing it well can be the beginning of getting the organization back on track. It is also a good practice for a new leader to do at any level.

UNITED WE STAND

Imagine an organization where everyone feels a strong sense of shared purpose, where people relate to one another in a way that fosters greater awareness of the work and of themselves, because they feel deeply understood and share a common purpose. They come together to form a common, compelling story, and they appreciate how each person's individual story fits into the greater whole. Through the power of their connections, they are able to push each other further to greater achievements. When things are tough, they help each other get through it, and that support creates an atmosphere that promotes reflection and growth. And when something goes wrong, they fix it. Together.

That kind of culture is not an unrealistic ideal. I see it happen in environments where leaders set the kinds of boundaries and structures that cause people to *attend to such dynamics and develop them, while at the same time inhibiting the things that keep them from happening.* And through continuity, they build a working memory of each other. But they do that because they have committed to building a culture that is united above all else, recognizing that a house divided cannot stand, but knowing there is no limit to what a united people can do.

QUESTIONS TO ASK

In what ways are your team and organization showing disconnection? What kinds of meetings do you currently have? Do they foster connection?

As you look at connecting better through meetings, what meetings do you need to add or discard to achieve that goal?

What barriers stand in the way of deeper connectedness right now?

Which "ingredients" of connection are missing from your team?

What is the biggest thing that you need to do differently as a leader to increase connection?

CHAPTER 6

THE GATEKEEPER OF THINKING

Pretend you are on a reality TV show where you are competing against another team. The team that produces the most revenue wins. You get to pick your team and lead it. Choose the right one, and you will get a big check from a guy who looks a lot like Donald Trump.

Which team should you choose? All the members of the first team flunked an aptitude test that was administered to gauge their sales aptitude, whereas all the members of the second team passed the test with flying colors. So which team do you want to lead?

Let's say you make the obvious choice: the smart guys who passed the test. With them on board, you implement all the great leadership strategies that you know. You cast vision, you communicate a great strategy, you set goals, you equip your people with sales training, you buy them the coolest presentation and marketing materials—you are leading to win! After all, you have the best team, right? You did pick the "smart guys."

But then the results come in. And guess what: you *lost*. And what's worse, your team of "smarties" has lost to a team of "dummies," who couldn't even pass a simple aptitude test. What, you ask yourself, just happened?

This story is not hypothetical (except for the reality TV part of it). It is based on a famous study conducted by Metropolitan Life Insurance Company and researcher Martin Seligman, as recounted in his book *Learned Optimism* (Knopf, 1991). This study examined the performance of more than a thousand insurance agents, comparing the results of those who had been hired based on passing the aptitude tests with the results of a group of agents who had flunked the hiring test. The flunkies won. Big.

How did they do it?

It turns out that there was another very important difference between the two groups of agents—aside from whether they could pass a test or not. The "flunkies" were *optimists*. And the smart guys they were compared to were not. The takeaway lesson is this: take someone who "can't" but thinks he can, and compare him to someone who "can" but thinks he can't. The positive thinker wins every time.

In this instance, the "low-aptitude," positive thinkers outperformed the "high-aptitude" ones by over 50 percent! How would you like to add that incremental number to your business? The way to do that is the subject of this chapter.

BOUNDARIES ON NEGATIVE THINKING

I like to tell people that "thinking" is like a piece of software. It is like a computer program that runs everything we do and dictates our outcomes. If a software program says do "a" or "b," then "a" or "b" will happen. If it is not written in the code, you can click on the icon all you want, but nothing is going to happen.

So it is with thinking in individuals and in groups. Whatever norms and behaviors get encoded and reinforced determine what happens next—indeed, what is *possible.* **The prevailing thinking patterns of a team or an organization—its norms and belief systems—will define what it is and what it does.** Not to mention what it doesn't do or what it doesn't allow for. And the leader's boundaries determine the thinking that prevails.

A well-known example can be found in the work of Harvard Business School's Clayton Christensen. In his book *The Innovator's Dilemma* (Harvard Business Review Press, 1997) he discusses how organizations deal with what he calls "disruptive technologies." These are new innovations that reshape the rules of competition in an industry. The impact of the new innovation or technology is often overlooked by industry leaders because to invest in the innovation doesn't fit their existing models and metrics. If the thinking of the company is "we can only do things that satisfy these ratios," or "have this level of returns," or are needed by "this many customers," then many new and promising innovations get overlooked or killed when they can't meet existing thresholds. The organization's thinking, and the practices and systems that reinforce these core beliefs, becomes so rigid and systematized that any new ideas are quickly rejected and alternative narratives are cut off.

But what if an organization encouraged people to think *differently*? In addition to existing metrics, what if they also had a way of incorporating different kinds of thinking into their daily routines? What if, for instance, their thinking included statements like this: "We will also *intentionally* try things that don't fit the current formulae"? This sort of thinking produces its own kind of optimism: "can do" thinking versus "can't be done" thinking. Tending to these sorts of thinking boundaries—the line between what is and isn't possible—is exactly the kind of leadership I'm talking about.

Look at your iPhone, or your iPod, or whatever device you use for listening to music. Do you notice that you have a lot of individual songs on there, but you do not have the whole album? Why is that? *It is because Steve Jobs rejected conventional thinking about how consumers would buy music.* Ignoring the negative, limiting way of thinking that "you can't sell a song one at a time," Jobs approached the music industry with a huge amount of optimism for doing something new. And that was that. You now can buy a single song in iTunes, and Apple gets paid each time you do.

Having read Walter Isaacson's biography of Steve Jobs, I can't imagine Jobs's confidence would ever have been shaken by a team of naysayers. But in many organizations, and with many leaders, that is not the case. They haven't effectively set a boundary and successfully prevented "it-can't-be-done" thinking from taking hold—in themselves, in their teams, and in their organizations as a whole. The reasons organizations get stuck in one way of thinking are manifold, but *one of the main causes is the failure of a leader to spot negative thinking and effectively set boundaries that prevent it from taking root while also making sure that optimism rules.* What you create, and what you allow, is what you get as a leader. Especially thinking.

THE "CAN'T BE DONE" VIRUS

I was working with a company where a team was considering an acquisition that would require a significant capital infusion. In the executive team meeting where the opportunity was being discussed, several members pushed back strongly on the idea: "We can't waste our time on this plan. It is impossible to get the financing that we would need to do this. We have to keep going forward with our incremental strategy, get revenues up, and then we can get the money. It is all about blocking and tackling. We just have to execute better." They gave reason after reason why no one would want to put money into their deal and why the supposedly hopeless effort to find money would cost them significant time, energy, and focus. "With our current P and L, there is just no way," Jared, the really smart CFO said, and everyone agreed.

I felt like my hair was about to catch on fire because I had just come from a meeting with another company whose founder did not think this way at all. In fact his company would not even exist if he had. When he had started it, he was in bankruptcy from a previous business. News flash: it is not very easy to get financing for a new venture when you are in bankruptcy, as your credit and borrowing power are nil. It would not have taken the smart naysayers very long to say, "Forget about finding money for a new start-up. It is not going to happen. Your financials won't allow it." But he did not suffer from that kind of thinking. Instead he thought it could be done.

So he found an office building for sale that he knew would be perfect for the right big tenant. Then he went to a Fortune 500 company and convinced them to rent "his" building (that he did not yet own) at a rent very favorable to them, *subject to* his purchase of the building closing. Next, he went to a bank and sold them on the blue chip company who had signed a lease with him that would more than service the note. The bank financed the purchase of the building, and he pulled $10 million out at closing and used the proceeds to finance his start-up. About six years later this start-up had amassed over $3 billion in assets—*assets created from bankruptcy, but not from bankrupt thinking.*

How many people do you think would have said to him, "You can't do that!" Most. And they would have sounded much like the team that I was listening to now, with Jared the CFO leading the negative charge. What concerned me about their exchange was that *this kind of negative thinking had become the operating system for the company at large and was keeping them stuck.* Their "thinking software" was driving the discussion that day, as it had been doing ever since Jared had joined the executive team. Virtually every meeting in the entire place was running that same "thinking software" that increasingly said "it can't be done."

Jared had been promoted to CFO when his boss had left for another company. He was valued for his smarts around analytics and for his ability to see things in the financial picture that Larry, the CEO, needed and could easily utilize. In a situation that had been complicated because of a complex merger and its subsequent integration, Larry had found himself upside down in the deal and dependent on Jared for his clear financial analysis. Jared had been a lifeline for Larry, and during the difficult crisis period, he had become his chief thought partner. Jared had helped him right the ship, and as a result, he had gained a lot of political and social capital. The downside was that he was also *affecting Larry's mind* and the mind of the rest of the team, in ways that had nothing to do with the integration problem he was helping to solve. The downside had much more to do with Jared's *general pattern of thinking*. And it was slowly becoming the thinking of the team.

I suspect Jared would have aced the aptitude test for Metropolitan Life, or any other test he was put to. He was a really smart MBA CPA. But *he was a negative thinker*. His own software would produce thought after thought that was limiting and negative. He always saw only the downside of the risk—what could go wrong and why not to move out of the security zone. But he expressed all this negativity in the most cheerful way, never "sounding" negative at all. He just would gravitate to the reasons why something could not work, though in a very nice way.

I first noticed this dynamic at an earlier team-building offsite I had led. Larry, the CEO, had hired me to help him build the new team, since some chairs had shifted at the end of the previous year. In briefing me about the team, he had been *very* positive about Jared, and I was quite impressed with Jared through his description . . . until I actually worked with him at the offsite. After the first morning of a two-day retreat, I racked my brain trying to remember anyone I had ever known who was such a downer. Jared was "nice," but—seriously—with every idea or thought that anyone had, his evaluation was Eeyore (from *Winnie-the-Pooh*) personified. But he did it so *cheerfully*. That was the sneaky part: a buzz-kill delivered with a smile. I was more than a little anxious when I realized I'd have to tell Larry that I thought his Superman was a Kryptonite vendor in a superhero outfit.

What was interesting was that later, when Larry and I talked and together unpacked the dynamic I'd first witnessed at the offsite, he realized how Jared had affected his own outlook, as well as the team's, ever since he'd moved onto the executive team. Larry realized that he'd become more cautious, overly analytical, and that he wasn't having "fun," as he put it. I had not known him before, but it was true that he did not seem like he was having fun now. He had attributed the change to the difficult time they had weathered. But I attributed it mostly to Jared—or rather, to Larry's adoption of Jared's style of thinking. And yet Larry was supposed to be the one who was "ridiculously in charge."

The team had made a similar shift as well. They were in the doldrums. They were just not energetic, and in their market *they should have been*. Things were hopping. In fact, the whole company should have been full of energy. But a fog of sorts had begun to take over Larry and his team. Gone were the drive and possibility that had existed when Larry had first taken the helm.

So back to the offsite: we began our work, and one of the projects was to come up with the *operating values* for the team, a common practice of mine. Even though the company had its values, I often like for teams to figure out the *team operating values* that will drive the behaviors that "drive what drives the business" (see chapter 8, "High-Performance Teams"). One operating value they knew they had to have was "innovation." So we went to work on that one, and I started digging to find out what was keeping them from being more innovative, even though they had the talent pool and the expressed desire to pull it off. They could do it if they *thought* they could, I figured.

Slowly, without naming Jared (because they did not even know that the negativity had come from him), they began to pinpoint the thinking dynamics that had infiltrated the team and the company. "It seems like we are afraid to make a mistake," one person said. "We analyze and analyze, and we do more and more research, but we don't pull the trigger," said another. "I think our risk analysis is not around the right metrics," another offered. "We are paranoid." "We need way too much consensus of too many people," was another. "We are too slow." "Too afraid to lose a little money," "Too afraid to get criticized by the board," "Need too much certainty before we take a step," and on and on the comments went.

Eventually the real Larry began to resurrect. "Well, I didn't come here to play defense," he said. "We are going to change this. We have to get this place moving." And he did. As we began to define the behaviors that would drive the value of innovation, they got their mojo back. The team started moving forward again. They had "attended," "inhibited," and exercised "working memory."

The kicker? Soon after they got moving again, pushing forward and taking some uncomfortable steps, including another difficult acquisition, Jared decided to move on to a different company. When I asked him why, he offered lots of solid reasons. But I think it was more than that. The reality, in my opinion, was that the team and the company were becoming too optimistic for him, and it was scaring him. So he left.

About six months later, the CEO and I went to dinner and were reflecting on how well the team was doing and how different the mood was now. He was profusely thanking me for my help, and I told him I appreciated his generous words, but I also told him something else about why things were so different.

"I think that everything is different because Jared is gone," I said. "And I think that Jared is gone because *you* are different. You stepped up and *put some boundaries on the negative thinking, and you created an environment where negativity could no longer live. You* did it. All I did was just help you to do what a leader has to do. And you did it."

He was "ridiculously in charge."

LEARNED HELPLESSNESS

Negative thinking is not just something out of some self-help book, encouraging you to "think your way to a new life!" As Seligman and many other researchers have shown, it has *real results in the real world, affecting the real bottom line.*

One reason is that anticipating outcomes, either positive or negative, causes different chemical reactions in the brain. Earlier we saw how the threatened brain works—indeed, how it freezes up and doesn't work as well as we'd like. In the same way, neuroscience researchers have demonstrated that the anticipation of a good outcome produces the chemical dopamine. Among other attributes, dopamine helps the brain be awake and interested, characteristics that are very important to performance and functioning. A positive and optimistic brain is a productive, energized brain ready to explore new ideas and to grapple with hard problems. That's exactly the kind of thinking leaders want to instill in their organizations. It's also why it's important to stamp out the negative. Remember: What you create, and what you allow.

As the case of the Wall Street brokers showed us, a crisis can really take a toll on people. And if you remember, it was not just Wall Street. I saw it in every company that I worked with during that time period. Most of the business world was feeling pretty down during the 2008–2009 crisis. But when I stepped back to examine what was really causing not only the brokers' distress and interruptions in their performance but also that of salespeople *and leaders* in several other industries I was consulting with, I was amazed by how their behavior mirrored a syndrome that has been in the literature for a long time, called "learned helplessness."

Basically you can think of "learned helplessness" as a change in the software of the brain that occurs when one of the most fundamental laws of the universe is interrupted in our lives: *the law of cause and effect.* We are designed to have a certain amount of control over our well-being. We do best when we are able to "cause" good things to happen to us, and to avoid things that would not be good. This certainty grounds our lives. We depend on it every day—the ability to determine our own quality of life in the smallest ways, and some of the largest.

Your brain first learns it in infancy. When you are hungry or in distress, you cry, and something good happens: someone comes with comfort, dryness, and food. Your brain learns very quickly that there is an order, or a set of rules, to the world, as in: cry and you get food. Or more generally: **Act and good things happen**. Through millions of other moments, this pattern gets reinforced, and you develop a life in which you feel like you have "agency" and "efficacy." Said another way, the logic is: "If my life sucks for some reason, I can do something to make it better."

In infancy I can cry for food; in adulthood I can get a job to buy a meal. If I have an itch, I can scratch it. Or if you hate that job, you can look for another one. If you feel lonely, you can call someone and go to dinner together. The operating principle we learn is: *do something good, and something good happens to you.* On the other hand, you can also avoid pain by *not* doing certain things. Stop banging your head against the wall and the pain stops. You are in control of both your pleasure and your pain. We depend on this law every day. Get out of bed, go to work, and get a paycheck. It really works . . . until . . .

> *we find ourselves in a situation where we are continuously affected negatively, and we have absolutely no control over the things that are affecting us.*

In that situation, you find that no matter what *you* do, the market around you still falls 50 percent. Your clients still lose half their portfolio. Your customers are not buying your goods. The economy still tanks and the newspapers still publish more and more bad news, fueling the already bad climate that you work in every day. And it directly affects you.

When this happens in a chronic, ongoing situation, the "software" changes in the brain, and negativity seeps in. And when you have negative expectations, a different chemical cocktail gets brewed in your brain. The result is not just a temporary sense of feeling like "life sucks," but a fundamental change in outlook and how experiences get processed. When such a change occurs, your brain tells you to basically "do nothing." Why? Because your brain thinks, "It won't make any difference." Your brain thinks that since you have no control over what is making you miserable, it might as well give up trying to have any control at all. How does this happen? To understand it, you have to remember what caused it in the first place: *a lack of control over things that affect your well-being.* The economy and the market conditions were affecting everyone's life, and there was nothing that they could do about it. It just was.

The perniciousness of this kind of powerlessness first came to light in research that subjected dogs to a small electrical shock. In the first part of the experiment, the dogs received a shock but could do nothing to avoid the shock. The dogs were then exposed to another small electrical shock that they could easily escape. *Nevertheless, the dogs responded passively and gave up trying, even in the face of this new option.* The first part of the experiment had taught them that they were helpless to act and to avoid suffering, and even when there was something they could do when they were given some control again, they had "learned" to accept their helplessness and do nothing. Put another way, their software had been reprogrammed: from "feel pain and do something" to "if you feel pain, there is nothing you can do, so do nothing." It is the same passivity that people often learn when they grow up in homes where they feel powerless. Even when they have grown up and have more choices, the passivity remains.

The big lesson for leaders is this: In a learned-helplessness situation, the brain can make a big thinking shift in how it tells your entire system to respond. It just goes passive and shuts down. Initiation stops. Creative thinking stops. The search for solutions stops. Problem solving stops. Trying new options stops. It's game over, or at least on pause. That is learned helplessness in a nutshell. Your brain thinks, "Nothing I can do." But, as if it could get no worse, it does. Later research showed that without some kind of intervention or reframing, this kind of passivity will become even more pronounced and predictable in a *thinking* style. Seligman put this thinking style into three categories, the "three P's," which are:

Personal

Pervasive

Permanent

The three P's are ways that people explain things that happen, and this thinking style shuts them down. It usually begins with a single event. Say a salesperson calls a client to offer a new product, and the client says that he is not interested. Someone with optimistic software would think, "Oh, well. Guess that client doesn't need it, or he has a brother-in-law he buys from, or he is an idiot, or has another plan," or some other explanation like that. And then the salesperson moves on and calls the next client, as if life is still normal and making calls leads to sales. But the person with learned helplessness thinks in a *very different way*, with the three P's now dictating how he experiences this episode.

He explains the event (the client saying no) very negatively in three ways:

1. First P: He "personalizes it."

Instead of explaining the reason for the "no" as something due to external events having nothing to do with him, *he explains it in relation to himself, in a negative direction*. "I am such a lousy salesperson.

I am a loser. I am not convincing when I talk to clients. I have no credibility. No wonder they aren't buying anything from me."

Bottom line: "It is because I am bad in some way."

2. Second P: He sees it as "pervasive."

Instead of seeing this as a *specific, isolated event*, just one client, he generalizes it to "everything." It goes from a single event to a pervasive reality. "It isn't just this client . . . *all of my clients think that about me*. In fact, it isn't just my clients. It is this whole business I am in, and the whole industry. And it is not just this product . . . none of our products are that good. And it is not just work. My friends really don't like me either. In fact, it really is my whole life. It's all bad." The single event has been interpreted in a negative way that pervades the whole picture. *Everything* begins to look negative.

Bottom line: "Nothing is going well."

3. Third P: He sees it as "permanent."

Instead of seeing this event as a single event in a single point in time, he sees it as permanent. He thinks it will continue happening this way. "It is not going to change. It will always be this way. The good days are gone. We will never make our numbers again," he reasons. The thinking says the current negative event is not something that will eventually pass but has become "the way it is, and the way it will be." It is the "new normal." *In short, there is no hope, and no reason to hope*. Once the time dimension of thinking becomes negative, the future is all but certain. "Tomorrow will be bad too."

Bottom line: "Nothing is going to be any different. So why try?"

So think about this formula and the implications for business. If people feel like they have no control over any outcome, and all of the outcomes are going to be negative, and everything about what they are doing is bad, and it won't ever be any different, because they are incapable losers and the market environment is hopeless too—then not much good is going to happen. They have learned that they are helpless and there is nothing they can do about it. What happens then?

They feel awful, their relationships suffer, and their performance tanks. Their brains change too. In the midst of the financial crash and the following year, I found this syndrome to be present in several industries, from real estate to financial services to health care to consumer products. The reality of the negative external situation, the financial meltdown, was rewriting people's internal software, and they were becoming very different people. Even previously high performers were being affected and acting as if there was nothing they could do.

Until . . . *they discovered they could rewrite the software.*

When we make this discovery, everything changes for the better.

It also explains why one salesperson may feel paralyzed and not hit his numbers while another colleague may have the best year of his career, *in the middle of the same bad market*. How does that happen? *They are thinking very different thoughts.*

The first one is thinking: "No client would want what I am offering because I have no credibility after the crash. Look at how my clients' portfolios are doing. I am not doing well at any part of the business, and besides that, the market is bad and it is not going to be any different tomorrow. This is just the way it is going to be." The result? Virtual inactivity, or low-energy activity, resulting in no new business, and no increasing business from existing clients.

But the second person starts to shift his thinking. It occurs to him that he has a couple of hundred clients. And a lot of them were not happy with him, *but it was not his fault, it was the market drop.* So he doesn't personalize the situation. Instead he has an aha moment: if any of his clients were upset with him, and potentially looking for a new broker, that means there are thousands and thousands of clients out there upset with *their* brokers and looking for a new one! (This was an actual discussion I had with a group of brokers. One had said that all of his clients hated him since the economic meltdown, and I just asked him, "So how do you think all of the millions of clients out there feel about their own brokers right now? Why don't you call all of them") All of a sudden, the world looks like a very, very positive place to be. The potential for growing business has never looked better. Lots of people are eager to make a change. Everyone becomes a prospect. As a result, he gets very busy calling and meeting people, asking them if they would be interested in hearing his strategies for surviving the downturn. His business begins to thrive like never before.

Same market as the first guy, very different outcome. The reason: very different software.

I saw this reality in the real estate industry. In one company I worked with, there was a leader who would not allow his people to think helplessly in the downturn. His team ascertained that people were not buying homes because their credit records had been so damaged by the downturn, and the potential buyers felt helpless themselves. So the sales force got busy and created a program to offer credit counseling as a part of their home-selling strategy; they found a way to help potential buyers clean up their financial messes so they could qualify to buy a home. Naturally a lot of people were eager to repair their credit scores, so they signed up for the program, and in the process they found that they could afford a new home too. The market was the same as before, but the company's results were different. Why? *They changed the negative, helpless program that had become their company's operating system*. Instead of being helpless, they got positive, and they got active.

And this was all because the leader set a boundary on negative, powerless thinking.

AUDIT YOUR OWN THINKING

If you believe there are some things that you do have control of, you *do* something. In the next chapter, we are going to see how that happens, and why you as a leader must be the steward over positive teams and cultures. For now, I want to remind you of what we said earlier: You are ridiculously in charge.

What that means is that if negative thinking is present in your teams, culture, and organization, *you are allowing it to be there*. So begin by taking a personal audit and asking yourself to what degree have you become a victim of negative thinking—your own and others. Has the market or any other force caused you to begin to experience any of the "three P's?"

> **Personal**: "What ever made me think I could be a leader? The reason we are stuck is that I am not up

to this task. What ever made me think I was good enough to pull this off?"

Pervasive: "It seems like everything I am working on is failing. Nothing is going the way I need it to go."

Permanent: "It is not going to change."

Some of these statements might seem extreme, but they are all examples of subtle variations that can linger in your head and still do damage. And as we discussed in chapter 2, your attitude and your way of thinking are contagious. If you think something can be done, then so will your people. If you don't, then neither will they. They will feel your energy and see your activity either way.

AUDIT YOUR TEAM'S WAY OF THINKING

After getting in touch with your own thinking, begin to look around at your direct reports, your team, and your culture. Do you hear negativity and helplessness? Just because you do not hear people talking about how bad they feel individually doesn't mean that *collective* learned helplessness hasn't become a problem. It can be present in individuals, but it can also be, and often is, present in the group at large.

For example, often we are looking for the P's when individuals think about themselves, like Joe thinking he is a loser. But if we only look at individuals, we miss a big part of the leadership opportunity, because the P's can exist in an organization as well. For example, the tendency to personalize can be heard in thinking like this:

> "Our brand is not as strong as the competition's."
>
> "Our product is not as cool as theirs."
>
> "We are so far behind the competition in R and D."
>
> "They are so much bigger than us."

Or in internal company examples:

> "Our division or department does not have the resources that Sales does."
>
> "My boss doesn't get it."
>
> "Management (or the owners, or the board) don't give us the resources we need to win."
>
> "I can't do this until I have more people."

Or the permanent virus:

> "Things won't get better until the economy changes."
>
> "Until the banks loosen up with money, we are stuck."
>
> "It won't change until our customers have more money."

When you think about it, each of these conditions could have truth in them. And you certainly don't want to replace learned helplessness with denial of reality. Instead you and your team must look at whatever external realities exist and begin to figure out a "non-helpless" response to those realities. There is always something you can do. And you as the leader must set a strong boundary against the tendency to greet any circumstance with learned helplessness. If half your clients are mad at you, make lemonade with the reality that the rest of the industry's clients are mad at them too.

No matter what obstacle your people face, they can beat it if it does not begin to make them feel helpless. Whether that happens depends on you and the degree to which you are able to set boundaries against pessimism and helplessness. If you look at the first set of statements above, for example, what you want to hear from your people is thinking that sounds like this:

"Our positioning is not as strong as the competition's, *so that means that we have to find new avenues to access.*"

"Our product is not as cool as theirs, *so we have to get busy revamping it and in the meantime communicate our value proposition through service and other offerings that we can do better than them.*"

"We are so far behind the competition in R and D that *we need a strategy to catch up. Let's turn up the steam on an acquisition and find some development partners.*"

"They are so much bigger than us, *so let's think about what advantages our size gives us and begin to capitalize on those and show our customers how our size is an asset.*"

Great leaders don't let their environments change them into helpless thinkers. When Martin Luther King Jr. had a vision of living in a country where color was no longer an obstacle, there was a lot in his current environment to be pessimistic about. Color truly *was* an unchallenged obstacle at that time. That was true. But he thought differently about the power to change that, and today we have a much different country. He did not buy into helplessness in the face of huge obstacles.

What you want to look for in your people is the degree *of active engagement they have with negative realities.* What do they do when things get tough? Are they passive? Do they go negative and become helpless? Do you hear "three P" thinking? Or do they actively engage? For instance, does their mind instantly begin to go into action, marshaling creativity and resourcefulness to figure out a way?

Even in the face of pessimism, you must remember that you are still ridiculously in charge and that you cannot allow that kind of thinking to permeate your organization. You must transform it.

FIND-A-WAY THINKING

It was the Fourth of July, and I was at a celebration that included a memorial "paddle-out" on surfboards in the Pacific Ocean, to honor and remember my brother-in-law Mark Metherell. Mark was a Navy SEAL, a great American, husband, father, hero, brother, and a friend. He was killed on a mission in Iraq in 2008. My ten-year-old daughter, Olivia, wanted to participate in the paddle-out to honor her uncle. So we borrowed a surfboard, and we began the walk to the beach where the surfers were gathering, with me carrying the board. I was excited for her to take part in honoring her uncle Mark, and I was inspired by her fearlessness in wanting to paddle way out into the Pacific Ocean with all the big people. She did just great, and when she came back onto the beach, we hugged. She was very proud and very thankful for her uncle Mark, and we spent a moment talking about all of it, before everyone gathered their things to make the long walk back up the hillside to the main event. Everyone, that is, except Olivia and a few other people who had decided to go back into the ocean to catch some waves.

She said to me, "Daddy, I want to stay here and go back out. I will come up to join you guys later."

"No, Livi. I'm sorry, but you can't. Who will walk back with you? You can't walk all the way back by yourself with just your cousin. Sorry," I said. I did not want her in all the commotion by herself at her age, and also, there was no way that she could get that big surfboard all the way back uphill.

"But it's fine, Daddy," she said. "There are some adults coming too, and they have to walk back. I will walk with them."

"No, Livi, just come with me now. It will be a lot less complicated," I said. Then I played my trump card. "Besides, the surfboard is way, way too heavy for you to carry back. They all have their boards and won't be able to carry it for you, and I can do that if you come now. If you don't come with me, how would you ever get it back up the hill?" At this point, I thought I had her.

But I had forgotten whom I was dealing with.

"Dad!" she said forcefully. "I will *find* a way."

Those words pierced my heart. I literally had to stop talking as I felt tears welling up in my eyes. It was true: she would *find* a way. Because that's who she is. The tears I felt were more than just a moment of being proud of her. The tears were that I literally, and I mean literally, felt something happen inside of me. At that moment, *I somehow got assured of her future in life.*

As a psychologist, I know that there are two kinds of people in the world. People whose circumstances overcome them, and people who overcome their circumstances. As the psychologist, I did not just hear "I will find a way to get the surfboard back." I heard something automatically coming from her innermost being, from the operating system that made her who she was—the kind of person who says, "I will find a way."

I knew that mode of thinking would serve her for life, no matter what her future circumstances might be. I knew that she will always "find a way."

"OK, Livi," I said. "Have fun."

"Bye, Daddy." And she waved as she ran to join the group.

I did not worry one iota, and in a couple of hours, she and the big heavy surfboard were back where they belonged.

As a leader, you won't have to worry either, so long as you are setting a strong boundary on negative thinking and building a "find-a-way" organization. You can put your head on the pillow at night and know that things are going to be OK. Why? Because you can know that your people, no matter what the market is doing or the circumstances might be, *will find a way.*

You will have made sure of that because you would have built a culture of optimism and proactivity. They will think that way because of what you have created and what you have not allowed. You will only hire those who think that way, you will train others, and you will make it impossible for those who don't to continue to think that way within your walls. You will set boundaries on any kind of thinking that says, "There is nothing we can do," in all of the subtle ways that it appears. You will not allow the "three P's" to exist, in any form. Instead you will proactively build an optimistic organization that believes it will succeed.

Research has revealed time and again that a belief that one will be successful is one of the strongest predictors of goal achievement. Great leaders build this belief into their people, teams, and culture. They believe that they can do it, and when things get tough, they *find a way*. They exert what I call "optimistic control," even in environments where there are many negative realities that they cannot control.

If learned helplessness is about losing the initiative and the grit to persevere, optimistic control is its opposite. It is about regaining proactivity, resourcefulness, and perseverance. In the next chapter, we will look at bringing optimism and a sense of control together. It is the formula for overcoming negative helplessness.

QUESTIONS TO ASK

Are there individuals you need to talk to who spread the virus of negativity?

How would you assess the prevailing thinking in your team? Organization?

Where are the places where you could make specific interventions to get rid of any negative or powerless thinking and increase active, positive thinking?

If the "three P's" of learned helplessness exist about the market or the company, how can you address that thinking specifically to a more proactive thinking about those realities?

Are there any individuals you need to talk to who spread the virus of pessimism?

CHAPTER 7

CONTROL AND RESULTS

When Tony Dungy became head coach of the Tampa Bay Buccaneers in 1996, the team had thirteen losing seasons behind them, and people were telling Dungy not to take the job. They said that there was no way to win. Dungy went anyway.

When he arrived, he heard lots of explanations for the team's dismal record. Some said it was because the stadium was old and the facilities were poor. Others blamed it on low ticket sales, which meant the team couldn't afford to hire the players that they needed to win. Others said that cold weather kept them from winning, as they never won games when the temperature was less than forty degrees. And then the kicker: Some fans mentioned the so-called Doug Williams Curse. Supposedly, some voodoo-practicing woman who loved Doug Williams, the former quarterback, had put a curse on the team when he left, and the team could not become a winner again until that curse was lifted.

As Dungy reviewed this list of obstacles, he realized something important: *the entire list was outside of his or his players' control.* He did not have the budget to recruit a bunch of superstars, and he didn't have the ability to build a snazzy new stadium. They couldn't control the weather across the country, and there was no way to get rid of the voodoo woman, whoever she was. Dungy was, in the language of the last chapter, facing things that he was "helpless to do anything about." Nevertheless, Dungy didn't succumb to the hopelessness that inevitably accompanies helplessness, and he didn't tolerate an attitude of helplessness in others either. *He immediately did something that all great leaders do,* and there is no way to minimize the power of this one move. Essentially he asked one penetrating question:

What factors do we control that will contribute to success?

He immediately went to work analyzing the statistics of the winning teams. He discovered that they shared three characteristics. They had lower turnovers (fumbles and interceptions), fewer penalties, and high-performing special teams (kickoffs, punts, punt returns). The first two characteristics have to do with what Dungy calls "self-inflicted wounds." Giving the ball to the other team, or having mental lapses or emotional eruptions that get penalized—these are mistakes you cause yourself. The final category, special teams, is one that is often neglected, but when functioning well, they create the big plays that contribute to wins. Dungy's strategy for winning boiled down to focusing on these three factors, all three of them totally within his and his players' control. He led them to a turnaround, and then he carried that thinking on to the Indianapolis Colts, whom he led to the championship in Super Bowl XLI.

The lesson for leaders is clear: *Focus your people on what they have control of that directly affects the desired outcomes of the organization.* When you do that, two powerful things happen. Not only do you get results, *but* you also change the brains of your people so they function better and then get even more results, in a spiraling, upward direction. Both are important.

REMEMBER THE BRAIN

Earlier we said that for the brain to be at its best, the executive functions of attention, inhibition, and working memory must be present. Then we said that a positive emotional climate, connectedness, and positive thinking add to the brain's ability to perform as well. Now we are adding another extremely important element to the recipe: **control**. A sense of being in control changes people's brains and affects their performance big time. Help them get a sense of what they can control that affects results and empower them to exercise that control, and you have brains firing with a lot of horsepower.

Here's what happens. When people's brains are working at their best, they are more creative, better problem solvers, less reactive, more proactive and goal oriented. They have more energy, and they have a better sense of well-being. The lesson for leaders is this: give people more control and they will thrive. And then, help them focus that control on the things that drive results, and they win, and you will, too.

It turns out that our brains just love control. When we perceive that we have the ability to be in control of things that affect some result, we get amped. It is the exact opposite of what happens in learned helplessness. Instead of powerlessness creeping in, it is intoxicatingly empowering, in a good way.

Neuroscience has shown that the more experiences we have of being in control, the better our higher brains function. *It is when we are affected by things outside of our control—and cannot regain a sense of being in control of anything that will make a difference—that we hit a real brain slowdown.* You can see why people who feel like they have little choice in life are more apt to give up, and go into negative spirals. But if they can regain a sense of control, great things happen. This is why leaders must turn into "control freaks"—just not in the way we usually think of. Instead of being a control freak by controlling other people, leaders must turn into control freaks about letting others be in control of what they should be in control of that drives results.

So great leaders do the opposite of exercising control over others. Instead of taking all the control, they give it away. They help people take control of themselves and their performance. The popular meaning of control freak is someone who tries to control everything, and drives everyone around him crazy. What I mean here is a leader who obsessively focuses on helping his or her people get back in control of *themselves,* to drive their own activities that directly affect outcomes.

BRAIN FUNK

I was addressing a sales organization in the aftermath of the financial meltdown and sharing my observations about the widespread sense of learned helplessness I'd seen crop up in numerous industries during those dark months. I explained why so many people were feeling down, defeated, and unable to perform at the levels they were used to. (It is amazing how just knowing that there is a reason for why you feel the way you do can be helpful. I wanted them to know that they weren't crazy.) But then, I heard the words that I never want to hear, especially from a salesperson.

"So, what you are telling us is that we are basically screwed," an attendee said. "If this economy caused this brain thing, then we are just going to feel this way until it is different." Then he uttered the words that I had come to loathe, as I had heard them repeated many times in many places: "This is just the *new normal*," he said.

I wanted to scream, but for some reason I was able to see the moment as an opportunity. "Yes, you are right," I said. "This has become the new normal. And that is exactly *your* problem."

"What do you mean?" he asked.

"Your aggressive drives, the energy that you summon to go out and win, have systematically shut down. Your brain has kind of quit. It feels that since you can't control the economy, you can't control anything. And now that you have been feeling that way for a while, your brain has *tricked you into thinking that that is the way it really is, that there is nothing you can do about it, and that you are truly screwed.* And it has become, as you say, 'normal' to think that way," I said.

"So we are screwed? We are going to feel this way?" he asked.

"No. I did not say that." I went on to explain that the thing he was calling the "new normal" was a *state inside his head.* "It has become normal to you to feel the way that you feel, and we really don't do much about trying to change what is normal," I continued. "So, since you now think it is normal, you think there is nothing you can do."

"That is how I feel," he said. "I just find myself not knowing what to do."

"Exactly," I said. "But if anyone knows what to do, it is probably you. You have been a leader at this company, and in this industry, for over a decade and a very high performer. If *you* can't figure out something to do, who can?"

Then I had them break apart into their teams to have them work through the exercise discussed below. When they did, their conversation quickly shifted as they got busy figuring out what they could control that would affect results, and began doing it. Really good things began to happen, not only in the business but in their brains, which was where it really counted. The trick was to reverse learned helplessness and get their brains moving again. I knew that if I did that, these veterans and superstars could figure out how to win. Someone was going to win, so it might as well be them, if they could get their heads working again.

In circumstances like this, the leadership mandate is exactly the same one Tony Dungy embraced: *find and focus on the things that you can control that affect outcomes.* And the good news is that when a sphere of control is reestablished—when boundaries are set to limit negative thinking patterns, on the one hand, and to identify the factors over which one does have control, on the other—learned helplessness can be reversed.

Remember the executive functions from earlier in the book? Attending, inhibiting, and working memory? Look at placing boundaries on learned helplessness in that same way. Dungy's team felt like they could not win because their stadium was old, the money was short, the weather was bad, and they were cursed. But his leadership boundaries set limits on that sense of learned helplessness by *attending to what they could control*: turnovers, penalties, and special teams. Likewise he *inhibited them from focusing on other things*, like Hail Mary passes, getting a new stadium, taking out voodoo woman, and hiring a superstar or some "wow" factor. And he *kept working memory alive as he kept his focus on turnovers, penalties, and special teams day after day with metrics ever before them*. As they did, they got better. And better. See the formula again? **You will get what you create and what you allow.** He created a focused sense of control and did not allow helpless thinking. And they started winning again.

REVERSE LEARNED HELPLESSNESS

There are a lot of ways of dealing with learned helplessness and negative thinking. In my work, what I have found to be very effective is to design a program that brings all of the elements we have discussed together in one powerful program. The results have been significant, as all of these elements are based on research of how people work and how their brains function.

This program is designed to help organizations get moving again—to reverse negativity and powerlessness—if they have fallen into that state, or to help good ones get even better. It is comprised of five components.

Create Connections

Regain Control

Take Note of the Three P's

Add Structure and Accountability

Take the Right Kind of Action

1. Create Connections to Deliver the Program

We have seen how connection works in chapter 4, so we won't repeat the particulars here. What I do want you to see, however, is that learned helplessness can be powerfully addressed in the context of a small, supportive team or group. This can happen with a few people, or more. Even in companies where I have literally taken thousands of people through this process in a system-wide approach, I usually divide them up into smaller teams to work together, preferably comprised of the work teams that already exist. A group of six to ten works great, but I have also seen performance turnarounds even when two people go through the program together. One woman in real estate turned her worst year ever into a successful turnaround just by *working this program with a friend* who was not even in her industry! But my preference is to have a number that is large enough so that there is a commonality of experiences, but not so large that there is not time enough for everyone to share their perspectives. (Research and experience suggest that sizes in the six-to-nine range are very effective.)

In chapter 4 I explained that relational support can change the brain chemistry and get the higher-order brain functions working again as threat decreases. It also helps when people find that they are not alone in facing obstacles, not the only ones feeling that way. It normalizes the struggle for them, allowing them to feel less threatened and defensive as they find out that others have similar feelings and experiences. As one man said, "I feel better already, just knowing that you guys are as screwed up as I am."

So figure out a structured time and space for people to go through this program together. And don't wait too long between get-togethers so that the impact of the previous session is lost. In my experience, results come pretty quickly, yet many teams like to continue these sessions for a longer time, using them as an ongoing mechanism for solving business problems and staying connected.

But no matter the frequency, it's essential that the tone stays positive in that it is about solving problems. That does not mean at all that negative realities are not discussed; in fact the whole process is about facing those negative realities. But the atmosphere and tone must be safe. Connectedness is built when the environment is safe, and when people are not just parading their strengths, or judging others, or hiding, but are being honest about their struggles. That is when the chemistry of oneness and unity begins to really take over and create group strength, when people are honest and willing to share their victories *and* their difficulties with each other. They have to get real and show some vulnerability. We bond with and follow people who are not perfect, yet are overcoming.

As a leader, you may choose to have someone else facilitate these discussions or you may facilitate the process yourself. In one company I worked with, we trained four hundred managers to take about ten thousand people through the program, so it can certainly be scaled, and you do not have to do it all yourself.

But if you are leading your team or others through it, don't think that you have to be above the fray. As I said above, research has shown that revealing some vulnerability increases connections, so don't be afraid as a leader to let your team know that you struggle with challenges as well. If they sense you are too far ahead of them in the battle such that they will never be able to catch up, they may not derive benefit from your insights. It's helpful for them to know two things: that you are overcoming obstacles and winning, but at the same time, that you are not immune or impervious to it all and have some real challenges. Think Indiana Jones: "I hate snakes," and then he wins in spite of them.

2. Regain Control Through the "Control Divide"

What I am about to tell you in this next step of the program is going to sound so simplistic that you might miss the profound value that it has. But you have to just trust me that its effects can be incredible for your business (not to mention other dimensions of your life).

It might help to think of it this way: when the doctor tells you to take a little pill, that is a pretty simple instruction. You do it, and you do it again at the proper dosage, and as simple as that is, the results can be amazing. Everything changes. You go from infected to healthy, feverish to normal, tired to energetic. Simple pill, simple instructions.

But the truth is that behind that simple pill there is a great deal of science. Biochemists and infectious disease specialists have spent years developing that pill. So it is with this "Control Divide," as I like to call it. It is a simple tool with profound effects. Here's how it works, for you and for your people as well:

First, take a piece of paper and draw a line down the middle of the page, creating two columns. In column number one, write down all of the things that you have no control over that are making your business difficult, such as the economy, the stock market, your customers' finances, the banks, your boss, the parent company, the health care cost increase, the company's overall budget, the board, the elections, the newscasts that hurt your business, etc. Those are the things that you have no control over that truly are affecting you. Get everything in that column that you can think of.

Next, I want you to REALLY worry about these items, even as a group. Obsess over them. Ruminate. Dwell. Think it through over and over . . . *FOR ABOUT FIVE OR TEN MINUTES*. Then, I want you to set the list aside until the next day when you can do the same thing all over again. The reason I suggest that you do this is that you *need* to! You need to worry about this stuff, and get into "ain't it awful!" for a few minutes because it is! It is really bad stuff. *I do not want you to be in denial.* Besides, your brain needs to complete the loop of making sure that *you* know how bad it is. Otherwise, it will continue to remind you of it, probably in the middle of the night or every time you have some good idea. So, focus on it. BUT . . . *only* for about five or ten minutes.

Next, after you have had your "worry time," I want you to draw a circle around that time block and *stop thinking about that column*. Quarantine it. Put a boundary around it. If you find it helpful, put a red STOP sign on it. No more thinking about those things.

Next, and most important, let's go to the second column. *In this column I want you to write down everything that you DO have control over that can drive results.* This need not be a final list. You can always add more activities as they occur to you and your team, as they probably will change as time goes on. But once you have the list in the initial form, I want you to focus on it every single day. *Make prioritizing and doing those activities the primary focus of every day.* Work the list.

What makes this simple exercise so powerful is that it speaks directly to our brains' executive functions *and* our desire to have control. The brain begins to "attend" to the actual activities that it can control (hold on to the football), and it "inhibits" the thoughts, behaviors, and information that interfere with positive actions (worrying and focusing on stadiums and voodoo ladies). The process of doing this, individually and collectively, builds up working memory and creates those positive, action-oriented behaviors that lead to better results, new products, new partnerships, new customers, and a lot more fun. The brain begins to get out of the mud.

Sometimes the initiatives are big and ambitious, but even the *simplest* initiatives can have a big impact. Consider, for example, one woman I met with at a technology consulting company at the worst moment in the financial crisis. I was doing the initial discovery process to figure out what was working and what wasn't. This person was thriving in the midst of the downturn while almost everyone else in her office was burying their heads and seeing diminishing numbers. What she was doing to thrive was exactly what I am describing here.

Here is how she explained her results: "Every day," she offered, "I come in, sit down at my desk, and look at that little yellow Post-it note on my screen. *On it I have listed all the things that I actually can do that I have total control over and will make a difference*: It says I can show up with energy and optimism—that is my choice. I can reach out to customers and find out how they are doing in this downturn and show them compassion. I can call them on a regular schedule to check up on them. I can do regular activities to create leads, and then reach out to a certain number of new prospects every day. I can craft an opinion on their consulting needs and communicate that to them, and I can give people a perspective on where this is all going for them to hang on to. I can offer workshops for companies. Each day, I can do all of those things, and when I just focus on those, I feel really good and good things are happening."

She was focusing on specific behaviors that she could control and that drive results, and she had managed to keep learned helplessness at bay. It's especially worth noting that her action steps were not amazingly creative. She was doing very simple activities and behaviors, the fundamentals, and they were working. As a result, she had a positive, hopeful attitude that generated energy that was very different from the kind of vibe her coworkers were giving off. When she talked to clients and potential clients, they were eager to listen and engage with her because of the positive energy she put out.

Optimism is powerful. But its resurrection cannot take hold until a sense of control is regained.

Over the course of working with many leaders in the midst of both good and bad times, I've seen all sorts of reversals in performance made possible once the leader and his team were able to reassert their control. One leader in a financial services firm held "town meetings" for clients that helped the firm regain their trust. As she told me, "I cannot control the market, but I can provide some stability with a community of people by consistently being there for them." Her business grew in the downturn as a result of doing this one thing she could control. She could do activities that built stability, and her clients responded.

A health care consulting company I worked with, in light of uncertain health care reform (over which they have no control and only limited influence), created a think tank of sorts to help educate customers about the coming changes. Although their future business model may be uncertain and they do not have control of all that the environment will demand, they do have control of how they interface with customers. And as they focus on that, they are beating their competitors, who are twiddling their thumbs and waiting to see how the changes will fall out before they "can do anything." They are partnering with their customers to deal with health care changes, instead of being victimized by them.

When you get your people to think about, look for, and take charge of what they can actually control, it has an impact on success. Brains change, and so does behavior.

I fly a particular airline often, one whose corporate culture is going through a lot of upheaval in a reorganization. And you can literally feel it as a customer. The gate agents and the flight attendants seem to be drenched in negativity, not only toward their customers but also toward their own employer if you happen to catch them speaking candidly. As a leadership consultant I am curious as to how the reorg is being led, so I often ask the flight attendants how it is going, and how they like the company. *In close to a hundred such conversations, I have not heard one single response that was positive.* The best I have heard is "we'll see." They seemingly feel very out of the loop, just being caught up in a situation they can do nothing about. Somewhere, somehow, employees have gotten the feeling that there isn't *anything* they can do to help make the airline better and contribute, thus helping the turnaround. They seem so negative, and de-energized, because the trap of learned helplessness is so powerful.

Of course, if they were encouraged by the airline's leadership to take control of what they absolutely do have control of, they might see a lot of simple things they could do that would add up to a very big deal. For one, they could smile. They could be friendly and proactively helpful. They could take an extra step to make passengers feel welcome and grateful to be on their planes. We would like that and probably choose to fly them more often. *They may not be in control of "management's" decisions, or the larger environment, but they are in total control of the customer experience for those few hours, which is the vast majority of time that their customers have interactions with their company.* If that message were being communicated and driven through the culture by their leaders, I am sure their employees would feel differently and those good feelings would trickle down to customer interactions too. That would turn into revenues, and they would then realize that they do have some control over what is happening "to them" in some of the cuts and concessions they have had to make. Companies making more money have more and better options with employees. It behooves both the leaders and the employees to realize this, and to be all on the same team, but it is leadership's responsibility to create that kind of realization and culture. Remember: **You get what you create and what you allow.**

In companies where employees accept a high degree of ownership for the drivers of the business that they can actually control, you can feel the effect. And there are too many forces in the business environment that you cannot control to ever give up the ones you can. Your competitors won't, and you cannot afford to, either. No matter what the larger environment, just like in football, both teams have to show up and play in the same rain. So take control, bring your rain game, and show up ready to play.

Great companies drive home this message every day and with every employee. They empower people to take control of the things they can control that drive results. The rest is just noise.

3. Take Note of the Three P's

Fortunately, ridding yourself of the three P's is not as hard as it may sound. It has to do with the simple practice, backed by research, of observing, logging, and refuting three P's thinking patterns:

Observing

Logging

Refuting

The way to turn around the three P's habit is to become aware of your own thinking patterns, first through self-observation, and then by writing these thoughts down in a log, journal, or notebook. Next, review each of the thoughts in the log and identify specific counterarguments and actual facts to refute them, one by one. If you think, "This call is not going to help anything," and you are feeling powerless to make it, refute it with a counterargument that says, "While not all calls lead to a win, many do, and the only way to find the good ones is to make the call. And if it doesn't go well, that isn't bad, either. I will have learned something. It is not horrible." In other words, write down the negative thoughts, and then write down a counterargument to dispute negative thoughts and statements, one by one. Grasp the counterargument and take action.

To illustrate how powerful this can be, in one training session I asked a participant to share with the group how the three P's were operating in his head. He said that when he makes calls, he has thoughts like "This customer is going to be angry that I bothered him with this call. He is bugged with me and the performance of my products already, and does not want to hear from me. He wants nothing to do with me, and it is not going to help to talk to him."

So I asked him to begin to write down all of those thoughts before each call and keep a log. I told him to put all of those negative thoughts in a column on the left. Get the crazy thoughts on paper. Next, write down a specific refuting thought, as I described above. Then make the call. After the call, write down what *actually* happened. Write down the *reality* of the call.

That turned out to be the real surprise.

He reported back to the group a few days later, noting with some amazement the wide gap between what had actually happened on the calls and what he had been consistently anticipating would happen in his negative state: "I was expecting the clients to see me as a bother, but many were actually glad that I was interested enough to reach out, because they were having some difficulties that they needed help with. We had mostly good conversations that led to some problem solving, and many agreed to get together next week. I have to say, I surprised myself."

Helplessness was reversed through awareness, counterarguments, and action.

When I had him continue to gather more data about his calls, he found that about 90 percent of what he was thinking was "crazy," in his words. He regained energy and turned his performance around. His fear and his inactivity went away. He began performing again.

But the real power happened when I encouraged team members to share their logs with one another. First, the group found that they all were experiencing some degree of three P's thinking, which helped everyone feel less alone with their fears and worries. Second, they found that their predictions about what would happen were wrong most of the time. As a consequence, they became more open, more objective, and more willing to engage in problem solving around actual problems and issues rather than getting bogged down in anxiety about what *might* happen. By replacing their old style of thinking (negative, highly subjective) with a new thinking pattern (objective, reality based), they were able to see opportunities instead of personal defeat. When the negative, global, subjective thinking was out of the way, they could treat each issue as a specific challenge and then figure out a strategy to overcome it. People can solve real problems. They can't solve problems with imaginary horrible monsters.

And remember, disputing negative thinking has two contexts: before and after. "Before" thinking is disputing the negative thinking that is keeping you from moving forward, from taking a step, such as the guy who could not make his calls. He logged his negative thinking before making calls, disputed them with specific counterarguments, and then took action:

The changes looked something like this, in terms of the three P's:

Personalizing Before the Call (or Action)

Old: I (or we) am not good enough to pull this off. It's going to be terrible. They won't like me.

New: I can take this next step, make this one call. I can execute it as best I can. Even if it does not mean a sale, it doesn't mean I am a loser, or no good, or that it is over. I can learn something from it for the next one and get better. It won't be the end of the world, and there will be a benefit. Each step is about getting better. I can do this.

Pervasive Thinking Before

Old: Everything is going south. Nothing we are doing is working, and this won't either.

New: Not everything is going bad. There are deals happening, and good things occurring every day. You won't find the good ones until you take the step, so get moving. Besides, there is more to my life than this one deal. It won't mean that all is lost if it does not work. It is one deal. So, get going. There will still be a lot of good when you look at the bigger picture.

Permanent Thinking Before

Old: It is not going to be any different tomorrow. It will always be the same as it is now.

New: Keep moving and we can change this and get to a win. The market always turns around. If I get active, I will be in position for when it does, and if it already is turning, I (we) will be there first. And, I (we) can be a force to turn it around.

By changing the three negative P's regarding bad self, bad total picture, bad future, to objective realities, the brain has moved from a subjective, global emotional state of "badness" to the thinking parts of the brain that treat individual events and problems *specifically* and realistically—as *objective problems that a creative brain can solve*. The brain cannot work on a generalized, subjective state of badness. But it can work on a *specific* action and treat it as a *specific* challenge with a positive attitude. Then, if it goes well, it can build momentum from there. And, if it does not go well, it can do the same thing after that it did before: *treat it as a specific event, not as a global conclusion, and interpret it positively.* So here are some samples of refuting the three P's *after* the event.

Personalized Thinking After the Event

Old: "I am such a loser and no good at this. I really screwed that up."

New: "That is one deal and it wasn't right for them. No one closes every deal or call, and a rejection does not mean that I am a loser. I will take what I learned there, use it on the next one, and get to a win. They had their own reasons for saying no. I am getting better each time."

Pervasive Thinking After

Old: "Nothing is working here. Everything is going in the wrong direction. And it is not just work, it is pretty much everything around me. It is my whole career and life."

New: "Not everything is going bad. There are deals happening, and good things occurring every day. You have closed some yourself and gotten some good new leads. You won't find the ones that will close until you take the step, so get moving. Besides, there is more to my life than this one deal. It doesn't mean that all is lost because it didn't work. It is only one deal. So, get going. There is a lot of good when you look at the bigger picture. A lot to be grateful for."

Permanent Thinking After

Old: "Things are really upside down and nothing is changing. It is just going to be this way, just like that one. It won't help to do anything, because the next one is just going to be the same. This is the new normal."

New: "That was one deal and I am going to take what I learned from it and go to the next one and figure it out. Someone is going to close a deal and it might as well be me. I (we) have the ability to figure this out, so let's take the next step and do it. People have to buy things, so I am going to find the ones who are ready."

One company I worked with had talked themselves into thinking that because their chief competitor had come out with a very strong media presence, they no longer had a chance in that market. But when they conquered the three P's—through observation, logging, and refutation—they saw that they had a lot more control over matters than they'd realized. They came up with a competing plan to tailor their offerings to individual clients, versus the mass media, and they went from helpless and hopeless to victorious. The individual focus was appreciated by clients. In so many cases, the reason for inaction and failure is truly all in the mind.

4. Add Structure and Accountability

Social psychology research has shown that when people assign a specific time and place for completion of specific tasks and goals, their chances of success increase by up to 300 percent. There is a big difference in saying "I am going to lose two pounds this week" versus "On Monday, Wednesday, and Friday, at noon, I am going to the gym," and put it in the calendar. The brain just works that way. Structure, stability, security, routine, and predictability—all are necessary for our brains to function at their highest levels.

That's why I encourage teams to get structured and accountable to one another in working on these issues. If you are going to work this program, for example, do it at a structured, planned, time for an agreed-upon number of weeks, as opposed to "when we can get around to it" or "when we have the time." In many situations, I have seen turnarounds happen as teams set aside specific times to work on defining their "what we can control" activities. They use these get-togethers to talk through what they can and can't control, process their negative P thinking, and then commit to getting back together, holding one another accountable at a specific time and place for executing their "what I can control" priorities. They hold one another accountable for working the action items in the second column. They are accountable for doing what they have decided that they can control that will have an effect.

At the individual level, creating more structure in order to turn around poor performance can be just as critical. In some instances, I've encouraged individuals, including some very high performers, to break their daily activities down to very small increments, sometimes as small as thirty-minute segments, and specifically plan what they would do in that time. It sounds pedantic, but it absolutely works. Having them write down their objectives for each thirty minutes of the day helps identify and isolate activities that are particularly endangered, due to inaction and three P's thinking.

You can see why that works when you consider that three P's thinking leads to a global, unstructured malaise. (Think how a depressed person can get lost in lethargy and let a day slip by without getting anything done.) Once specific actions get identified and assigned a specific time, the person is able to focus on reversing his inactivity and get moving, which builds confidence and momentum for tackling other tough tasks as well. Create structure though specific time assignments for your structured (column two) actions.

Now, if you are the kind of person who feels imprisoned by "structure," not to worry. I am not suggesting that everyone has to do all of this "for the rest of your life." Rather, it is specifically designed for when some sort of "learned helpless" dynamic has set in. It's a way to jump-start a different dynamic in people's functioning. But I would also add that once people begin these practices, they very often continue to use them in some form long after the initial stuck-ness has been resolved. Try it in full in the beginning for you and your team, and then adapt it once you are out of the woods.

Nothing moves people like moving. In learned helplessness, goal-oriented action has virtually stopped, reinforcing the negative mentality, so just getting movement can begin the turnaround. This is one of the reasons why this structure is so powerful. But two more things are important to get the ball rolling: first, the *right* kind of action, and second, the *right* kind accountability.

5. Take the Right Kind of Action

By "right kind of action," I do not mean mere activity. Busyness is not action that builds momentum or results. *The action you want is action that specifically drives results.* And the accountability you want is the kind that drives success, not the kind that only measures results and keeps score. Many people measure results, such as sales. To be sure, hitting revenue targets, making sales, and growing marketing share are absolutely critical measures that must be monitored for accountability. But they don't necessarily *drive* success—they only measure them. What I'm talking about is accountability that *creates* high performance and results. Figure out what that is, and you will undoubtedly see winning results as well. Said another way, don't count the score. Count the behaviors that run up the score.

Remember Dungy. His metric of accountability wasn't winning a Super Bowl; his metric was turnovers, penalties, and specialty team stats. If each week the players were focusing on and being held accountable for how many times they dropped the ball, threw it to the other team, or for how much yardage was given up on a punt, *they were measuring the activities that would eventually lead to outcomes,* that is, a winning season or a shot at the Super Bowl. As is so often the case, winning the Super Bowl was a result of Dungy's focus on the right metrics of accountability: the ones that *drive* the result, not just the result itself, such as the final score of the game. So should the case be with yours.

In the list of actions that your people can control, have them find the ones that *actually affect outcomes*. How many calls to clients are they making each week? How many presentations did they make? How many acquisition targets did they uncover? How many due-diligence plans did they complete?

If they are managers, how many coaching sessions did they hold with key reports? How many branch visits? How many confrontations of poor performance with their reports did they do? How many reviews of progress on strategic plans and tactics? How many trainings? The key to success is to be expending energy on the actual drivers of results, not just actions in general.

It is not just counting how many sales you make, but counting how many calls you make. That is what is going to end up making sales. Then as teams are coming up with those drivers and counting them, and setting targets with specific deadlines together, or with whomever they report to, *they can be held accountable together for the right actions.*

Also, peer accountability, out in the open, is very powerful. Within a group of people it gets tougher and tougher to give excuses and explanations based in learned helplessness. Only action counts, doing what you have told them you would do. And then only action that drives real outcomes. A group sees through the fluff, especially when they are involved in doing the real stuff. And if you are in a team with shared goals, there is even greater positive peer pressure to perform, as the group needs you to.

Even teams whose roles are not directly tied to generating revenue should know how their actions are aligned with and drive the results of the company. They need to know exactly how they contribute and how they will be made accountable for their efforts. While flight attendants are not the ones who sell big air travel contracts to corporations, when they smile and deliver a great experience to customers, think of what happens. Those customers on the plane are the ones who will be choosing the airline that their company is going to fly with. So even though the flight attendants are not in "sales," they certainly are in control of actions that indirectly drive revenues and results. Believe me, if I did not have so many miles with the airline I mentioned earlier, I would be tempted to move to the one where employees smile.

A POSITIVE ENERGY FIELD

Change requires energy, and producing it is one of a leader's greatest jobs. Learned helplessness, and its concomitant negative thinking, suck energy right out of an organization. A leader must set very strong boundaries against helplessness and negativity; he must also provide the fuel to get people moving. Getting people to attend to what they can control that affects results, while inhibiting activities and thinking that don't, is one of the most powerful ways to create energy where there has been stagnation.

I will close this chapter with one more example. A residential real estate developer I worked with was in a very bad market situation, and neither he nor his competitors were selling much of anything. One of the important metrics in this business is the cost of carrying a project until it is sold, carrying the loans before the finished property can be sold. The longer a project takes to sell, the longer the builder has to carry the cost on his books, and the higher the costs eating into profits. Therefore, time-to-closing is a key driver of success. As you can imagine, any CEO studying the numbers will be eager to move inventory.

In this instance, the CEO had delivered a clear message about what factors his team could control to beat the competition, and drove that message continuously. "You can control three things: have the best product, have the best salespeople, and have the best price," he had told them. They could not control the recession, but those three they could absolutely control. Having delivered on the first two, product and salespeople, and still not getting sales, he saw that the only one that was left to attend to was *price*.

What had happened up until this point was that their competition was lowering prices when there were sales in the marketplace, trying to catch up with others in the price drops. In the CEO's mind, that was reactive. The only way to get ahead of the price war, he figured, was to do one thing before anyone else: forget margins and focus on *closings only*, and drive the result by activating a behavior that you can control: *lowering price first, and by a lot*. In the short term, margins would be lower, but you would win in many other ways in a bad market. So he gave his team one target mandate that they could control: "Make closings, period. Cut the price to make closings, but make the closings. *And he put them totally in control of meeting the closing metric by controlling the only behavior that would drive the closings—lowering the price.* They were free to lower it to make a close. And they won, big time, beating all the competition and not playing catch-up. They stayed ahead of everyone else, ended up cutting prices less in the long run because they were first, and got rid of expensive carrying costs. In their markets that year, they were the only builder that did not lose money. They focused on what they could control, and held each other accountable for closings.

They had been stuck and depleted of focus and energy—until they started paying attention to *what they could control that drives results*. Injecting people with energy and a new sense of power and control is a huge part of what leadership is about. You can set values and goals, but if you give your people specific ways to be in control of actions that drive the organization forward, you'll have created a distinct competitive advantage.

QUESTIONS TO ASK

How much control do you think you give to people in your team and organization, making them feel empowered to affect results?

What are some contexts or relationships where you see the program to Reverse Learned Helplessness applicable? Where have people gotten helpless in the way they are working and thinking?

How could you implement the program and its different elements of connection, control, and changing thinking, structure, accountability, and action?

What did this chapter say to you most about leadership?

CHAPTER 8

HIGH-PERFORMANCE TEAMS

OK, in the spirit of getting the dead fish out of the drawer, I have to tell you that no matter how long he has been here, and how much loyalty we have toward him, Jerry is just not able to oversee moving a factory from one country to another. He just can't pull that off." So said the head of operations at the beginning of an executive team meeting.

If you were a visitor to this particular conference room, you might wonder what in the world this guy was talking about. Did someone named Jerry leave his sushi in the desk drawer the night before? And why would that disqualify him from heading up this project?

On the other hand, if you were a member of this executive team, you would have known *exactly* what he meant. His reference to "a dead fish" was shorthand for a lot of hard conversations this executive team had tackled to get to this moment. A dead fish? They got it.

So, what was it that the team instantly understood? It went something like this:

Talking about Jerry's ability is an issue that we all know is not pleasant. It smells bad.

And even though it smells bad, no one wants to deal with it. So it stays hidden in the drawer. As a team, we have committed to always getting the dead fish out of the drawers. In light of that, we are now going to talk about it, and I can assume buy-in from you guys.

After a few heavy sighs, the team got down to it. Jerry had to be reassigned. No doubt about it.

If you are really confused at this point, I understand. Let me take you back a few years with this team, and it will become clear how "dead fish" entered the team's vocabulary.

AN EXAMPLE OF "STINKY" TEAMWORK

When I first met the CEO of this global retail electronics company, he had asked me to help him build his new executive team. He had just been named CEO and wanted to do some team formation. I explained to him that my view of team building was that it required more than just relationship and communication skills. While those are important and can bring a team closer together, sometimes that kind of team building does not carry over to the real work that the business needs to do. When I think of team building, the relationships and communication must be connected to creating high performance as well.

Nothing drives strong teams like great performance, and what drives strong performance is a commitment to a shared vision and shared goals with behaviors and relationships aligned with reaching those goals.

Teams can get along well and still go nowhere; to get somewhere, they have to do more than get along. They have to work together on the right things in the right ways at the right time toward the same goal. They have to perform. And that requires teamwork. And teamwork is only driven by a shared purpose or goal.

So I told the CEO that I wanted to focus on the team's real work and on the kind of team they would have to be in order to match their vision with real results in the real world. What kind of team would it take to do that? *That* is the kind of team that we needed to work on building. And, yes, they should also communicate well and like one another. That really helps too.

So we set up a series of offsites, and I gave the CEO an assignment to take to the team: "I want you guys to come to the offsite with four case studies of your business. Two that went really well, and two that went really badly. They can be anything you want, but I want them to be large enough to have involved either the entire enterprise or the entire executive team."

"OK," he said with a somewhat pained smile. "That won't be hard. . . . We have both good ones and bad ones for sure."

"And one more thing," I said, "assign a reporter for each scenario to give the narrative."

He nodded and we parted.

When we all got together I asked the first reporter to tell us the first story. The scenario was a product launch gone bad. They were a couple of years removed from it, so it was both recent enough for all of them to be very aware of what happened, but also far enough removed for them to have gotten some objectivity about it.

In a nutshell, here's what had happened: in the desire to beat competitors to market with a new product, a lot of things had broken down. For one, the marketing and sales group had made promises to customers and to their own retail stores about the availability of certain product features without checking in enough with the development team who actually had to make the stuff. When the engineering team finally learned what had been promised to customers, they were none too happy, to say the least, and noncommittal about whether they'd be able to add these new features so late in the process. The result? A sales organization primed to deliver product features that they had been selling, which would not exist, at least not on the timetable that they had promised. And a development team, its hackles raised, willfully resisting how important it was to adapt their design to accommodate customer feedback. They were divided.

Long story short: the product was late to market; the company's largest customers were mad about that but equally upset that the features they'd been promised were nowhere to be found; and bad reviews in the media followed shortly thereafter. The company paid the price for the team's meltdown, which was all the more maddening because it wasn't for lack of skills and talent, and it wasn't for lack of a "plan." It was for lack of a team that could work together as a team to get the job done.

They had not failed in their related *business* functions, in any technical sense. They had failed in their *team* functions. They had failed at the number one thing a team has to do: work *together* to accomplish a result that none of them could do alone. That is a team.

TROUBLESHOOTING A TROUBLED TEAM

As the memories of this experience came back to life for the team, I asked them a question: "What team operating values, had they been in place, would have prevented this from happening?"

"What do you mean?" the CFO asked.

"Well, let's say that the team had some specific values that actually drove *behavior* among the group. Values that dictated how you work together and also prevented you from working in other ways that would allow this bad result to happen. What would some of those be?" I said.

"How would we figure those out?" someone else asked.

"Well, let's look further into your story, and see what actually took place in this launch. How you guys *behaved* and how you *worked* to get this result, and we will see," I said.

So they did. They did a thorough autopsy of the whole product launch, from conception to delivery. They looked at timelines, how decisions were made, who was involved and who wasn't, the criteria of some of the decision models and risk analyses, the planning and execution, and on and on.

It became obvious pretty quickly that everyone had known there were problems, but there was no moment when the team had truly come together to address them. Problems just kept getting pushed back and forth between the two factions, like—you guessed it—a "dead fish shoved in a drawer." After all, who really wanted to be the one who said, "We can't get there in time?" When the pressure from the CEO was always to hit the numbers, the "dead fish" was "anything that smelled like we won't reach the numbers." The smell had been growing throughout the process, because no one was willing to openly say, "This will not happen."

And what about delivery on the specific promises that had been made? And accountability for the lack of delivery? Here too the team was able to recount the many ways in which both internal promises to colleagues and external promises to customers were not kept. Even more troubling than a lack of "delivery" was that *nothing really happened when an internal or external "deadline" was not met*. Indeed, deadlines were missed so often that missing them became expected—the "new normal," as it were. Delivery was defunct, and accountability, in a word, was kaput.

As the team continued to relive this worst-case scenario, I filled up flip charts with all the elements of the story:

> Numbers pressure that prevented the negative conversations from openly occurring.
>
> Individuals going away from meetings and conversations with very different understandings of what was happening and what could be expected.
>
> Conversations that mostly were about "convincing the other person."
>
> Very, very different agendas within the departments and absence of alignment on what was important to each.
>
> Avoidance of the issue when they all knew it was there.

The interesting thing about this list is that it looked almost exactly like the list we put together for the other stories the team shared: the same patterns, the same problems, albeit with different details and specifics. That is what I usually find: a team has its "ways" of working, no matter what the project is. And in those instances where a project matches well with the team's ways of behaving and operating, things go swimmingly; but when it doesn't, things start stinking up the drawers. The exception is that sometimes outside circumstances are such that a team is forced to work in different "ways" than its own, and because of that good fortune, it succeeds. An example would be when they do a joint piece of work with a different company or a different team that utilizes better patterns of behavior and practices than their own. These isolated, good outcomes can lull the team into complacency, as they think those successes were because they are good, when, in fact, someone else made up for their gaps and weaknesses. They had a chaperone.

CHANGE BEHAVIORS = CHANGED OUTCOMES

But now, with the flip charts on display for all to see, the team's failures and successes stared right back at them. That can be overwhelming, but it can also be enlightening. Then, when you ask the right question, it can also be empowering:

"So, do you see anything up there that is not in your control?" (Remember . . . you are "ridiculously in charge.")

They looked at the sheets. None of the reasons for their bad outcomes had to do with knowledge or skills they didn't possess, nor with forces, such as a bad economy, outside their control.

It all had to do with behavior.

And the one thing we know about behavior is that it is under your control. When you recognize that fact, you can move from being overwhelmed to being empowered. You realize that everything that causes bad outcomes is in your control to change, and that everything that causes good outcomes is also due to your behavior. *Change behavior, and you change outcomes.* That is power. And *empowering.*

As a next step at the offsite, we began lumping the elements on the flip charts into categories. What emerged was the answer to the original questions that I had asked them:

> What values and behaviors actually drive the results of your business?
>
> Which ones cause good things to happen and prevent bad outcomes as well?

Together they came up with a group of values that, if lived out, would drive results and prevent disasters.

That is what values do, if indeed they are true operating values that lead to behaviors that lead to results. Otherwise, they are just placards on the wall. As we discussed earlier, **leaders get what they create, or what they allow**. So, a team's operating values create a certain kind of environment with an allowance for certain kinds of behaviors and a prohibition against others.

Which brings us to another point. *Values make it possible for a guiding language to develop that gives structure and identity to the boundaries of behavior we want to encourage and prohibit.* Every team needs a common lexicon, a memorable language, to communicate just what these boundaries are. When the team landed on the saying "dead fish out of the drawer," everyone now knows exactly what that means. And whenever it is said, the team instantly comes together around a shared value they had agreed upon. Everyone begins to listen. One team I know has a phrase "give me the last 10 percent," which is a way of telling someone, "I don't want you to hold back on what I need to hear. Tell me the last 10 percent that is hard for you to say." Once they hear that, freedom to be totally honest comes, thanks to a common language. The language drives behavior.

More about language in a moment, but let's get back to this team. I won't take you through how all of their particular values were derived, as you get the point of the process by now, but just to give you an example of the great values they came up with for their business that would have prevented the "bad results" and ensured the "good results," here they are:

Communicate to Understand: *We seek to thoroughly understand and be understood.*

We engage in respectful, collaborative, TIMELY, and complete dialogue. We clearly and directly convey ideas and share our point of view, while maintaining openness to different perspectives. We listen to understand and respectfully question to achieve clarity, IN BOTH MESSAGE AND MUTUAL EXPECTATIONS. We openly discuss critical issues, and deliver difficult messages with care. WE COMMIT TO NOT LEAVING IMPORTANT THINGS UNSAID AND WE AVOID SAYING THEM TO SOMEONE ELSE OTHER THAN THE PERSON WHO SHOULD HEAR THEM.

Urgency on the Vital: *We take action on what's important.*

We CONTINUALLY differentiate between what is vital and what is merely urgent. We set clear, strategically aligned goals and focus on execution of priorities while balancing short- and long-term business needs. We proactively remove barriers, solve problems, and prioritize to ensure the vital work gets accomplished, WITH A CONTINUAL PRESS TOWARD BOTH DEFINING AND EXECUTING THE VITAL.

Global Awareness: *We understand how being a global business impacts our work.*

We continually develop our understanding of the global opportunities and challenges associated with our business THROUGH TRAVEL, INCLUSION, FORUMS, SWAPS, AND GLOBAL COMMUNICATION, and build this knowledge into the decisions we make and the work that we do. We partner with our colleagues around the globe, SHARING AND leveraging our cultural differences and knowledge, to successfully compete in global and local markets. WE ACT AS A GLOBAL CITIZEN.

Customer Intimacy: *We build customer relationships that guide our success.*

We approach our work with an understanding that the customer is the reason that we exist as a company. We intentionally build strong collaborative relationships with our customers, recognizing that by deeply understanding their needs and providing solutions to help them, we will continue to profitably grow. WE DO THIS BY LISTENING, CREATING, AND FINDING VARIOUS TIMES, WAYS, AND CONTEXTS TO INTERACT WITH THEM, BOTH IN THEIR WORLD AND OURS. WE MAKE SURE THAT WE SHARE ALL THAT WE KNOW ABOUT OUR CUSTOMERS WITH ALL OF OUR PEOPLE.

Connected: *We partner with our colleagues to achieve results.*

We collaborate with colleagues across functions, sites, and regions. We actively identify those who need to be involved in a decision or project and bring them in at the appropriate time. We build trusting relationships across the organization that break down barriers and help us to achieve our goals. We proactively share information and best practices to increase the success of the organization. WE SERVE AS EACH OTHERS' RADAR, FLAGGING THREATS EARLY ON AND COMMUNICATING THEM QUICKLY.

Deliver: *We do what we say we are going to do.*

We hold ourselves accountable to our responsibilities and fulfill our commitments. We recognize that in a dynamic environment, our priorities may change and when they do, we proactively renegotiate commitments with stakeholders and communicate our realigned focus. We make timely decisions and use learning from past experiences to continuously improve our ability to perform, INCLUDING MATCHING, COACHING, AND DEVELOPING TALENT AND BUILDING THE CAPACITY NEEDED TO DELIVER ON ALL MILESTONES.

Build Our Talents: *We continually develop ourselves and others.*

We value the talent and contributions of those we work with AND WE WORK WITH UNITY AND COMMITMENT EVEN WHEN WE DISAGREE. We partner with our colleagues in addressing challenges and celebrating successes. We strive to grow our own knowledge, skills, and abilities and enable others to do the same BY MODELING, DEVELOPING EACH OTHER, AND GIVING FEEDBACK RESULTING FROM CONSISTENT OBSERVATION AND INVOLVEMENT

WITH OUR EMPLOYEES AND THEIR PERFORMANCE AND NEEDS.

DEFINE VALUES THAT WILL DRIVE RESULTS

As this list illustrates, great values *must be connected to the business and not just empty platitudes hanging on a wall somewhere.* For example, the value of Global Awareness came from the other case examples discussed at the offsite, where many of the business practices fit the United States and Europe but did not fit the other countries into which they had expanded, with results suffering. This company's strategy involved growth in much of the rest of the world, so when processes, products and upstream marketing, and design coming from the United States (and the West Coast in particular, as that is where they were located) did not always fit other countries, it became apparent why they were getting some disappointing results. They saw that the behaviors and practices driving many decisions were too United States–centric, and they realized that to win as a global company, in every meeting at the highest level, they had to be sitting on top of the globe, not hovering over the western United States. Otherwise they would make decisions that could end up hampering global efforts in significant ways.

Similarly they became aware of how many times the sales and marketing group, who spent a lot of time with customers, felt like they were trying to be advocates for the customer with others who were not on the front lines. Much of what they were trying to get across felt like an uphill battle. And it made real differences in the results, as some things that customers wanted were often voted down because of other metrics. So they decided that Customer Intimacy should be an entire team value, not just driven by the sales and marketing group. If they were truly going to be about the customer, *everyone* had to live and breathe the realities that their customers lived, and then there would not be big disconnects between R and D and sales, or between sales and customer service. They committed to finding ways to get everyone closer to the end user experience so that they would not split in that discussion but all come from the same reality.

My point is that teams need a *results-based method to determine which values and behaviors fit the real needs of the business.*

Team building must be done not only with relationships in mind but also with the real drivers of the business in sharp focus.

Good relationships are essential, but teams also have to accomplish a very specific vision and mission. They have to *perform*. To do that requires not only values that drive the correctly aligned behaviors that drive the business, but also values that prevent behaviors that limit or hurt the business. Add accountability practices to that and you have a jet engine for a team.

A team is not a "group of people." A team is a group of people who have a shared purpose or goal. The shared purpose or goal brings them together to perform to reach that goal. And to reach the goal, the team is going to have to look and operate in a certain way. The team's values and value-driven behaviors are going to make that goal a reality.

The job of the leader is to form that team around a common purpose or goal, and then work with the team to figure out what that team is going to have to value and behave like to reach that goal. When that is done, a leader has created what is needed, and not allowed what will prevent the purpose or goal from becoming reality.

QUESTIONS TO ASK

What operating values have you and your team developed that connect to the drivers of results in the business?

What do you need to do to lead the process of defining those operating values if they don't exist?

To what degree is the team working on aligned and shared objectives versus working on their own objectives?

What do you need to do to get them to a shared objective where if one wins they all win and if one loses they all lose?

What do you need to do to establish team covenants around specific behaviors?

What can your team do to hold one another accountable?

CHAPTER 9

TRUST MAKES TEAMS ABLE TO PERFORM

Recently I had an enlightening conversation with a CEO client about his work with his team. He had just a few weeks before taking over a new business unit with about $500 million in revenues. As the new leader, he was amazed by the disorganization and lack of clarity he saw. Sometimes, just from the disparate amount of work, he would just sit in his office utterly confused as he tried to figure out what triggers to pull to get the organization moving. There seemed to be so much to do, and yet so many fragmented parts.

My first suggestion was to divide the business into two areas of focus with two questions:

What were the immediate, short-term activities (remember those execution functions: attending, inhibiting, and working memory) that were required *in order to make the quarterly numbers that the investment bank and the board were demanding*?

Second, what were the activities that were required to *get the business on the path of positioning it for the longer term that would drive its growth and build its value for the expected returns on investment past the near term?*

Focusing on just two specific categories gave him instant clarity. That is what executive functions do; they illuminate the path forward, and inhibit others. So, he went to work on those.

In our next meeting he shared something really powerful that he had begun with his team to get them attending, inhibiting, and remembering. It was exactly the kind of practice I mentioned in chapter 2. He had installed two monthly meetings to keep his team attending to, as he put it, "the data in front of them." (attend, inhibit, working memory) His first meeting was organized around this question: *Is the business healthy?*

When I asked, "What do you mean by 'healthy'?" he said, "There are two parts to healthy and how I define it for them to focus on. First, is it 'predictable and shapable'? Meaning, from a planned-results standpoint, are we getting what we said we were going to get (i.e., predictable)? And for the specific reasons we thought we would (i.e., shapable)?"

He continued: "So, first, we go through all of the key indicators and metrics and try to figure out where it appears out of control, i.e., where are we not getting the results we said we would, or not doing what we said we would, or things not happening as we predicted they would happen. Then, if we are not getting the results we said we would, we go to a root-cause analysis to diagnose 'what is the cause of that?' If the expenses were not what we said they would be, why not? If we said we would hire someone to drive something by a certain date and didn't, why not? If we said that we would sell *x* or *y* and didn't, then why didn't we? If we said this amount of marketing would produce this amount of sales in this region and it didn't, why not?

That will tell us what we can *shape* [remember my earlier emphasis on what you can control] and how to make corrections to shape it better next month. If we are not predicting results well, then we have to do the things to shape different results. That leads us to health. It forces us to ask, 'If something we expected to happen did not happen, how do we fix this so it won't surprise us again?'

"But then we go past that . . . and this is huge: the fact that we did not predict well, and did not shape well, has caused a *gap* in our plans and budgets. If we predicted that the hire would have taken place and it was going to add value, we have to admit and own right now that there is a gap in our plan that is going to catch up with us if we don't do something about the gap created by this problem. Said another way, it is not just about fixing it for next month. It is also about fixing the new problem that we now have because of what we *missed* last month. . . . It really keeps us attending to what we need to attend to, inhibiting what we need to not have happen, and keeping it all in front of us all the time. "

Talk about an executive functioning with executive functions. This is it!

The CEO continued: "One of the great things about this meeting is also for me to observe to see if any of my people is surprised by the information in the indicators. If they are, and they are not already aware of where those indicators are in their departments, then I know they are not running the business. These are the numbers that each one should have a *working memory* of all the time. The meeting is to fix it, but they should already be aware of all of this stuff. If not, they are asleep at the wheel."

Then he said this about the executive functions of attending, inhibiting, and working memory:

"When we talked about the concepts of those executive functions (attending, inhibiting, and working memory), it all became so clear how my last business worked and now what I needed to do with my current team. Get them attending, inhibiting, and having a current working memory of it all. This meeting is an example of a way I thought of to apply it."

He had said that he has had two meetings, so I then asked about the second one. Here is what he said:

"The second meeting is about getting them together as cross-functional resource owners and making sure they are *aligned around the top handful of key initiatives that we have going on.* As a business, if there are five or so key initiatives that we have said are the most important, like a product launch, a revenue thrust of a certain product, a region, a continuous improvement project or a customer interface issue, or whatever, those tend to go across all functions. So I have them prioritize them together *as a team* and *allocate their resources to one another around those initiatives.* 'If these are the five top things for us, and here are the resources needed to get those done, what resources are they going to need from each other in giving each other people, teams, focus, etc.?' Real teamwork. The key here is to see that the team is aligned around a **shared purpose or goal. It does not belong to a person, but to the team as a whole. As a result, it is going to take the entire team to make it happen. That is the essence of a team.** As a result, you will begin to see collaborative behavior.

"They begin to say things like 'OK, I will need these guys from your group for a week to drive this or that to make it work," etc. They have all agreed to the shared priority, and they know that they all have to work together to make it work, so that is what drives them to do that 'for each other,' as it is really about what they *all* have to accomplish as a team goal. They have to give to each other to get there. You don't hear 'I can't spare giving you that guy' as much.

"What it does is huge in that I cannot personally track all of the deep stuff in each function that really matter in the business, but they can do it together. This way, even though I can't get deep in the weeds of all of it, I can make sure it is getting done. It is a great attending focus."

Very, very cool, I told him. What a great example of attending, inhibiting, and working memory, *but done as a team*. It was a great example of getting the functions loaded into teamwork. I told him as he shared this example that I would have to include it in a book on the executive functions of leadership in a team, as it was such a great illustration of how it works, and we laughed. But then he said something else that brings us to the real point here, which is "trust." He explained,

"But as powerful as all of that is, it would never have worked if we had not done all of that earlier work on the culture of the team, especially 'building trust.' "

"I agree," I said. "Trust is the starting point and makes it all work."

"And you can see why you *especially* have to have a lot of trust in these meetings," he said.

"What do you mean?" I asked.

"Well, those discussions are difficult. They get to hard topics, looking at whose part is not working, what ideas failed, which efforts are contributing, etc. That can be hard to say and hard to hear. And especially the second part about working together and allocating resources across functions to each other. They commit to making sure that initiatives are truly resourced across functions in ways that cost them personally sometimes. They are really working *for each other.* They are giving up their own agendas for the good of the team. That only comes from doing the work on the culture of the team, and having really, really high trust with each other. They can say what needs to be said, receive it well, and hold each other accountable. That requires a lot of trust, and the work we did a while back on trust paved the way for this and enables it to happen," he said.

He was right. When they trust one another, they know that they are *for* each other and *for* the shared interests of the team.

Can you imagine trying to get a team to allocate resources within their group, *for* the group, without trust? Without alignment in a shared purpose? Too often individual agendas and functional silos stand in the way. But as we saw in the beginning of the chapter, if they have decided what kind of team they need to be, and what values are going to dictate their behavior, then they will have been working on the kind of trust that can make this kind of alignment possible.

So, how do you get to that kind of trust?

The only way is to work on it proactively and diligently. And in my experience it takes two components: first, a good *definition* of what trust is, what it means to the individuals and the team as a whole. Second, agreement on how it is going to get *executed.*

GET AN AGREED-UPON DEFINITION OF "TRUST" FOR THE TEAM

In working with teams, I begin by talking about the nature of trust itself. What is trust made of? What are the elements that have to be in place for us to trust someone, or a group of people? Psychologists, business theorists and practitioners, relationship experts, and others have written on trust for decades and more. Here are some of the components* that I think matter most:

Connection through Understanding

Motivation and Intent

Character

Capacity and Ability

Track Record

Trust Grows When We Feel Understood

The first requirement to build trust is to connect through understanding the other person. Remember, people do not trust us when we understand them. They trust us *when they understand that we understand them*. What that means is not "that we get it." What it means is that "they get it that we get it." For that to happen, we have

* These components are written about in my book *Integrity* and also in Steven M. R. Covey's book *The Speed of Trust* (New York: Free Press, 2008).

to listen and understand where they are really coming from, and truly connect with them, showing them that we understand. So that they know they have been connected with. That takes time and attention. They need to *feel it*.

That requires that we provide a space to get to know them, make it safe enough for them to be vulnerable, and show us what things are really like for them. In a team, that means that there is time and attention given to understanding each person, their function, what drives it, what makes it difficult, and so forth.

Here is one example of what can happen when we give time and space to work on trust. It comes from an offsite I did with a team desiring to build more speed and agility in their company. My diagnosis was that a lot of their problems stemmed from an emphasis on "consensus," which often caused people to not really say all that they meant, and which made getting to an actionable decision take far longer than necessary with everyone trying to be so "nice." If only they could just get together and say what they really meant without fear of offending someone.

I told them they were going to have to build more trust at two levels. They had to be able to trust each other to really say what they were thinking, *and* they had to trust each other that if they said it, it would be well received, even if disagreed with.

So I had them go around the table and answer some questions. First, "What are your fears about telling your teammates the truth, or giving them feedback that might be hard to hear?" Second, "What are your fears about receiving that kind of truth or feedback?" I asked them to share an example of a time when it had gone particularly well, or particularly poorly, and how they would like to get truth and feedback given to them. The results were fascinating.

Some talked about times when getting good, clear feedback had literally changed their lives or careers, as hard as it had been to hear. Others described times when the news had been delivered in very destructive ways, and what had happened to them as a result. It was very moving in several instances, and there were a few moments where someone got choked up.

One woman said that although she knew critical feedback was good for her, and wanted it, she was so afraid of it that she had asked the team to first "say that you still like me and I'm not getting fired, and *then* tell me what's wrong. I need the reassurance." We all laughed and then she said, "I'm not kidding!"

Another guy said, "I am the opposite. I want it straight up—right between the eyes. I don't want to have to guess about it. Let me have it so I know what to work on."

A third said, "When you give me feedback, I need you to understand where I was coming from when I did whatever I did. I can't stand to be not understood. You can tell me anything you want if I feel like you know where I was coming from."

A few things stood out. First, their perspectives were all different. It surprised them to hear the many different thoughts and experiences that had shaped them. And it helped them immensely to get to know each other at this level around something so important. They began to appreciate each other's communication styles and vulnerabilities. Second, it helped them know what each of them needed in feedback and difficult-to-hear truths, which prevented future hiccups, as they knew better how to deal with each other.

But third, and perhaps most important, *it helped them get to a team operating value around trust*. Here was the key discovery: When we looked back for common threads, it was clear that the fears of telling others the truth, and giving hard feedback, greatly outnumbered the fears of receiving it. They all *desired for others to give them the hard truths. And yet, even though they wanted it for themselves, they were all afraid to give it to each other.* In other words, there was a roomful of people who were afraid for no reason! They wanted it, but no one was giving it! They were fearful of giving feedback for no reason, since everyone desired to get it. All unnecessarily walking on eggshells.

So through understanding where each other was coming from, hearing their fears and experiences, they found a way to be more straightforward with each other, knowing that it was desired. They *trusted* that it would be desired and received well, and they did not have to hold back. As one person put it: "Talk about making faster decisions! Now we don't have to have three more meetings to get to the nugget of information that is holding the whole thing up that someone is afraid to say with everyone present. We can rock and roll, now that we know no one is taking it personal. Let's go!"

But the implications of trust go much further even than just having open communication. It goes to the heart of the team's work and the company's operations themselves. Think of it like this: When a doctor really understands your life, he is better able to prescribe the right treatment. And when you really understand that he understands you and what you need, you are more likely to comply with that treatment. Then you are working together because you trust him. So it goes with trust in teams.

I remember once, in a team meeting with my staff, when I gave an employee a project to do and a deadline. She told me there was no way she could do it. I disagreed, countering that it wasn't that big a deal. In fact, I was certain she could get that project done in time without it taking away from the other objectives I had committed her to. She pushed back again, and I was bugged. I thought she was being negative and exaggerating the whole thing. From my vantage point, it was all very simple, very much a just-do-it proposition.

As the conversation went on this way, I could tell she was getting amped up, even though she was not getting overtly mad. But I saw her chin trembling, not in sadness, but in anger. Her words were getting crisper and almost staccato as she said them. Then she said, "OK, come here. I want to show you something."

We went down the hall into her office, where she proceeded to outline all of the work that had been required the last time I'd asked her to take on a task very much like this one. Wow, I could now see, it was complicated and time-consuming, involving interactions with federal agencies, professional agencies, and several businesses. The paper trail alone was daunting. I looked at her and said nothing for a moment. I was embarrassed at my clueless lack of understanding.

Finally I just looked up and said, "I'm sorry. I had no idea."

At that moment, I saw a few tears forming in her eyes. She finally felt understood, as she understood that I understood.

We returned to the larger meeting and took a fresh look at the plan and timeline we'd been working on before. As we talked, there was a different energy in how she was looking at it. She was engaged in trying to figure out solutions in a different way, almost pushing us to do more. The physics of our interaction were different. *She was no longer moving against us, namely me, because she knew I understood her.* She did not have to protect herself anymore. She trusted me, so she could stop resisting me and join me instead. Plus, as she described the things that were involved, I was not resisting them and was more in a role of working together to find some solutions.

Trust Grows When We Know Someone Intends to Help Us

There used to be a saying that the definition of a bad day was when Mike Wallace showed up at your door. Anyone who had ever seen *60 Minutes* knows that when he showed up unannounced, the intent probably was not to help grow your business. He was there to expose something wrong. And usually you would see the people run for the hills, avoiding him and the cameras.

"Intent" is key to trust. As I said in the book *Integrity*, if we know that someone's intent is to help us, that they are "for" us, we open ourselves to them. We give to them. We cooperate with them. We invest in them. We share with them. We work, and even die for them. But if they are not "for" us, there are only two other possibilities. They are "for" themselves and neutral to us, or they are actually "against" us.

In my book *Integrity* I wrote about intent and the importance of being "for" someone in order to establish trust. One example I gave was about my dealings with a person who was honest, and reliable, and would never lie, cheat, or steal. But when asked by a friend whether he should do business with him, I hesitated. Basically, I told the friend that the other person would not lie or cheat, and could be "trusted" to do what he was contractually bound to do. But, I added, "Whatever you need, make sure you have him contractually bound to have to deliver it. Get everything you need in writing. Because he is not going to look out for your interests past what he has to, and especially if it gets in the way of his."

That's what I mean by "for themselves," and "neutral to you." They are not necessarily out to get you; they are just trying to please themselves and their own agendas. To truly trust someone, *we need more than that.* We need to know that they are looking out for us as well as for themselves, and thinking about how things will affect us, especially when we are not there to look out for ourselves.

Contrast this example with a CEO I know who found out that the benefits package for employees was going to cost less than they had budgeted for. Instead of just reducing the line item on the budget like his benefits VP wanted to do, he said, "We have planned for this cost, budgeted for it, and we can afford it. It was always for the employees. So let's take the extra money and put it toward their retirement funding." He was the kind of person who was more than neutral toward his employees. He was "for" his agenda of making a profit, and he was also "for" his employees, representing their interests even when they were not present. They had no voice at the table—oh, wait—yes they did: they had *his.* That is the intent of being "for" the other side. He was "for" them and his intent is for their best, even when they are not present. His employees trusted him implicitly, virtually never left the company, and gave their all to the company for decades.

When teams truly realize that they are "for" each other, and that each member is "for" their shared objectives, then they trust each other. And—this is huge—*they represent the team downward in their own functions or departments.* They wear the "team hat," instead of the "functional hat."

One of the biggest problems in organizations is when members of the executive team represent their functions at the table like members of Congress representing their home district, arguing for resources and protecting constituents. There is nothing wrong with looking out for your people, but that is not an executive team. An executive team, or any other team with a shared objective, has to wear the "team hat" first, and then represent the shared team objectives throughout the organization.

I just spent a few days with a CEO of a $6 billion company who fired his very competent CFO and told him this: "Here is your choice. You cannot be CFO. The reason is that you are concerned about finance, your vertical department, but you are not concerned as much about the "horizontal," meaning the entire company across all the verticals. The 'whole.' I need people on my executive team who are about the 'whole company,' not only about their own function and not only about their own people. So you can take a different position where you can learn to care about the horizontal, or I will take your resignation now. If you could learn to care about the horizontal, I think one day you could be an incredible CFO."

That is what I mean by the intent and motive being for the "whole" and for the "other" as well as for oneself. That builds trust.

Remember my client's second meeting, where the team came together and committed to each other the resources that they had to share with each other across functions in order to make everything work? They had to be "for" each other, "for" the team, and "for" the enterprise in order to reach the goal. So when they went out into their own departments, they had to represent those shared interests of the team, instead of talking smack about "those guys over in marketing." That is what it means to have the team hat on, and not only the hat of one's own function, department, or self.

Trust Grows When We Display Credibility and Character

It is virtually impossible to get around talking about character when talking about trust, even though it seems harder to pin down than more easily measureable kinds of performance. It is real nevertheless. You know a character problem when you see it, and your guard instantly goes up.

Character encompasses a wide range of attributes—from morals to ethics to personality traits, attitudes, and ways of behaving. For instance, if someone is impulsive and leaps into action before they do their due diligence, we would not say that is a moral character issue, but it certainly is a pattern that we see in the person's makeup that affects their work. Or, if someone is a poor listener, or is a political maneuverer, or is domineering, we would not say they are of "bad" moral character, but we would say that there are issues about their makeup that affect the team. That is what we are talking about here . . . the person's makeup that we see operating in a consistent way:

Blind spots

An inability to connect with others

Being more of an individual contributor than a team player

Managing one's own career more than the interests of the team

Not being able to deal with negative realities—failure—or criticism

Having an aversion to risk and always gravitating to the secure path

Lack of discipline

Poor or indirect communicator or "yes" person

These are all examples of people's makeup that are not moral or ethical per se but that *certainly* affect results. My way of thinking about "character" is that it involves a person's "whole" makeup, not just "moral." The real meaning of "integrity" is about being a "whole" or "integrated" leader. (For more about this topic, see my book *Integrity: The Courage to Meet the Demands of Reality*. New York: HarperCollins, 2009).

On the other hand, when people exhibit other character attributes—a willingness to listen, to seek the truth, to persevere, to try to be wise, to take calculated risks, to work for the team over their own interests, sacrificing and serving, to be disciplined, and to be kind and understanding—we trust them. We move toward them and will give more of ourselves to them and want to serve them. We know that it will be worth it. Sacrificing for a person of good character, investing in them, always accomplishes something good, while lots of effort can be wasted on people whose flaws are significant enough to make our investment fruitless.

It all goes to having credibility. As dictionaries say, credibility is about "believability." A person's character patterns give them credibility or believability in a certain domain. Recently I was working with a company where the leader was scheduled to address the entire company about a strategy initiative, and the executive team called me and said they wanted to get together to talk about his not doing the speech. The reason? They said that he would have zero credibility around that initiative. It was so counter to his patterns in that area that they said it would take people further away from the goal than it would help, just because they knew him so well. They would miss the message because of the character of the messenger.

So, in a team, it is important to first of all choose people well.

Choose the ones with the good character that is matched to the behaviors and the outcomes that you need to have. My Navy SEAL brother-in-law, Mark, was matched in his character for the missions that he was asked to perform. Courage, perseverance, high-team skills, discipline, high pain tolerance, and other similar qualities made him perfect for his work. You can bet that there are many talented people who do not make it through SEAL selection because they lack the makeup that is necessary for the realities they will face. When choosing, think of the realities that your business must face and choose well in terms of character.

Trust Grows When We Believe in Someone's Capacity and Ability

Another factor influencing trust is someone's capacity to actually do what we trust him or her to do. Someone can be very connecting and understanding, and have a really good intent toward us, but still not be trustworthy to do something specific because they don't have the capacity to pull it off. They are not "bad" for that, but we can't entrust certain parts of the mission to them, as they just can't pull it off.

Do not trust me to do brain surgery. Even if I understand you, and have a good intent, and have good character, I will probably remove the wrong lobe, and every time you blink your right leg will kick. Or worse. But if it comes to understanding and helping you with your leadership issues, I am a better bet. I do have abilities in this domain that are utterly lacking when it comes to brain surgery (even though the two activities sometimes feel like the same thing).

With teammates, we do well to talk through issues of what we can trust each other to do and what we can't—and then to help each other rise to higher capabilities over time. It is OK to talk openly about what we really think we, or someone else, is able to pull off and deliver. You can say that, if both of you know that you are "for" each other.

Is your team specific about their fears about each other's capacity? Can you have enough trust to say "I am not sure that falls into your strengths, Terry. Let's talk about how that is going to work." And does Terry have enough trust to know that your intent is "for" him and the team and the organization when you say it? Can he thank you for giving him that gift?

When a team has this kind of trust to enter into capacity discussions, they find the gaping holes in their teams and put an end to long-standing patterns. They either add the capacity by bringing more talent to the team, or they develop one of the members. Capacity must exist, but it takes trust to get there, and then you can trust it to deliver.

Trust Grows When Someone Has Built a Good Track Record

I was visiting a small town in southern Louisiana and asked for directions to the restaurant where an event was taking place. The lady I talked to told me to continue down the road I was on for about five miles, take a left at the first light, and then keep driving. "When you see the big dog lying there, turn right, and go another two miles. It will be on your left."

"Excuse me . . . a dog? Lying in the grass?" I asked.

"Yessir. He'll be right there on the right, lying in the grass next to the culvert. Just turn there," she said.

"Uh, how do you know the dog will be there?" I asked.

"Oh, he's always there. Just turn when you see him," she said.

This had to be the strangest set of directions I had ever heard, but I had no other choice, as this was before phones had GPS. I set out and followed her instructions.

To my utter amazement, when I took the left and kept driving, scanning the right side of the road, there he was: a big shepherd-looking dog just lying there in the grass, right by a drain. I could not believe it. No one around, no leash, no dog pen. Just lying there. I turned right, went to the party, and could think of little else.

How did she know he would be there? A dog? She knew he would be lying next to the road? Really? How?

The only way to know would be if you had been down that road a few thousand times, and every time you go by that corner, there he is. The dog has a track record. He has a past. He is dependable. He has done it before, without exception. And if he has been there thousands of times before, chances are pretty good that he will be there today. If he isn't there, he probably died.

Said another way, we can trust people to do what they have done in the past. Or another way, the best predictor of the future is the past, unless there is some intervention that has made things different. That is a track record.

If the team is going to trust someone, that person is going to have to build a track record of bringing results in some area. Of performing well in that ability. Of delivering well in what has been promised. Or at least having delivered in ways that would logically make sense to trust her in this new way.

Then there is also the "team track record." Teams need to look at their own track records as well. When they want to pull something off, they are going to have to ask, "How well have we done at this in the past?" If you look back at the beginning of this chapter, that is what I was asking that team to do. To look at its patterns, its track record, to see what issues they need to address. And in the example I gave earlier of my client's monthly meetings, that is what he is doing as well. He is asking his team to look at their track record of predicting and shaping the business, and make adjustments so that in the future they can trust what they are doing better. When they can trust their ability to predict and shape, then they can confidently make bigger investments.

Investment is always driven by trust.

WE MAKE INVESTMENTS WHEN WE FEEL TRUST

When you think about it, that is what we are looking for in life. *Investment.* We want people to invest their hearts, minds, and souls with us. We want our teams to be invested in what we are trying to build. We want individuals to be "all in." We want friends and loved ones who are invested.

And where do we make investments? We make investments when we trust that someone's intent is for our good. We trust when they have the character patterns to make us believe that they will behave in a certain way that we know is "characteristic" of them. We trust them when we know they have the capacity to pull off whatever we are depending on them to do. And lastly, we trust when they have a track record of good results and positive behavior. Add all of those together, and we want to "invest." We want to place what is of value in their hands. We want to place it in their "care."

In fact, to trust really means to be "careless." Think about it. If you put your money in the bank, you are careless about it. You don't have to "take care" every day to make sure that it is safe with that bank. They *understand* that you need it available to you on a moment's notice. They have the *intent* to keep it safe and earn you interest. They have the *trustworthiness* of honesty and integrity. They have the *capacity* to keep it safe with armed guards, FDIC insurance, and substantial deposits. And they have a *track record* of never going belly-up or experiencing a run on the bank where people could not get their money. You trust them, and you do not "take care" of your money. *They* do. And as a result, you can be "careless." You sleep at night not worrying about whether or not it is safe. That is why you invest it with them.

When we trust each other in a team, we can be careless as well. We do not worry whether or not the other people on the team have our best interests at heart. We do not worry whether or not they have the shared interests and goals of the team at heart. We do not worry about their character, or about their capacities. We do not have to watch our backs. We believe in them. And we know their track record. As a result, we *invest ourselves*.

For your people to invest in the team and what the team is trying to accomplish, you must work on building trust proactively through defining it, and then diligently through executing it. That gets us to the second point about trust: executing it.

EXECUTING TRUST THAT LEADS TO PERFORMANCE

Earlier I noted that trust is built in a team by two things. The first is to define it, to mutually understand the elements and the anatomy of trust itself. The previous section gives us that anatomy. Connection, intent, character, capacity, and track record are the building blocks of trust. The next question is how to form a team around those elements. How to execute it.

To "execute" means to "produce in accordance with a plan or design." So if you are trying to produce a team that has high trust, how do you produce it with a plan or design? There are many methods, but here is a path that I have found very helpful that takes trust to deeper levels of becoming an aligned, results-oriented, accountable performance team.

Define Trust

Define Your Shared Objectives as a Team

Define Operating Values and Behaviors That Will Get You There

Utilize Case Studies

Make Specific Covenants for Behaviors

Develop Accountability Systems

Put In an Observing Structure

Define Trust

We talked about the dimensions of trust above (connection, motivation, ability, character, track record). To execute those, take that list of elements and talk about them in the team. Go through each one, and get everyone talking in the way I described above. Take one of the constructs, such as the "connection through understanding," and ask a few questions: "How well do you think we understand each other?" "Let's talk about safety in this team when talking about the hard issues. How safe do you think it is? What gets in the way of that? How could we make it better? What is hard for each of you? What would you like to see different?" etc.

Go through all of the elements and have the team work through them. Where do we need to feel like everyone's motivation and intent is really for the team? For the company? For the results? What are we doing that gets in the way of that and makes it feel like our intentions are really not "for" each other? How can we change that? Or, "How is our track record around this or that issue? How has each of us performed? What can we do better to encourage more trust?" Most of these that fall short will not be "intentional" sins. It is just that people think about their own world most until they get together and think above their own interests intentionally, and all together.

Define Your Shared Objectives as a Team

Much of what we have talked about has to do with the shared objectives of the team. That is the real definition of a team, accomplishing a *shared* objective or goal. One that cannot be accomplished by any individual apart from the rest of the team. Otherwise, it is just the pooling of individual accomplishments and adding them up, like a scavenger hunt for revenues. A team is a group that *has* to work together to get a *shared* vision or goal accomplished. The CEO I mentioned above who fired the CFO who did not work "for the horizontal," was emphasizing the importance of the whole working together. One of the mantras that he said that he drives into leadership over and over is that they all win together or they all lose together. "There is no such thing as one of you winning but the whole thing losing. We are in this together." So they learn that there are no individual victories or individual losses. We win and lose together.

To get there, the team must come together to get clarity on exactly what those goals are. What are they trying to do *together* that takes all of them to do? I recently worked with a retail chain's property group who were responsible for finding locations for their big box stores, designing them, getting them permitted and built, etc. Each function in that group had its own department, but they had to begin to work together as a team to handle their growth and rapid expansion.

They had had some difficulty working together before, as the group that was finding locations defined success as the number of new locations they were finding per year. But the design group was graded on how good and market sensitive the design was to drive sales. The two groups had, in their minds, *very* different functions that could work against each other. You can find and build a store pretty quickly if you don't care about the design, and you can care so much about the design that it slows down construction substantially, working against the top-line revenue growth.

So they had to get to the purpose of that team that was a *shared* purpose, which had something to do with the higher purposes of the overall business itself, which would include both of those, speed of construction *and* quality of shopping experience. When they realized that was their goal, not speed *or* shopping experience, their behavior changed and they started to design with speed of construction high in mind as they also built with stages of design in mind. That is having a shared outcome. Then they could work on this question: What is it going to take from each one of them to get there? How did they need to behave for each other to get that done?

Define Operating Values and Behaviors That Will Get You There

Make sure you are clear on the shared objectives for this team. In terms of values, ask your team a few questions:

What is this team's collective purpose? What do you want this team to accomplish?

If that is what you want to accomplish, then what does this team need to look like in order to pull that off? How does it need to operate?

What values will bring that vision to reality? How do those values relate specifically to the vision, goals, etc.? How will they drive them?

What behaviors will demonstrate and drive those values? How do we need to behave to make sure it all happens?

That gets them thinking about important things related to the results they are trying to drive, like the case studies above. If they are going to be adaptive to a changing market, for example, they might realize that they need to have the value of "speed," with the ability to make quick informed decisions. OK, if that is true, what behaviors are going to drive that value? And so on.

Then they can begin to look at how they work presently and how they need to change their behavior in order to be the team that can accomplish what they have decided they want to accomplish. In Coach Dungy's language, you can't win a Super Bowl if you are a team that drops the ball a lot. So how can we be a team that doesn't do that? What do we need to do to make sure we do not drop the ball and throw interceptions?

If you are a business that needs speed to make your vision come to fruition, what behaviors and practices do we need to do that will ensure speed ? (For Coach Dungy, this might be holding on to the ball.)

Utilize Case Studies

Go through a few case scenarios, good and bad, and ask yourself these questions: What values would have prevented the bad outcomes from happening? And what are the values that made the good outcomes occur? When did we win and why? When did we not win and why? Those questions will help you to see the ways that the team works when it does well and when it doesn't, and you can figure out the values that you need to keep the bad outcomes from becoming patterns.

The interesting thing is that depending on the business and the objectives, different teams can have very different values. For example, one team may need "high connection" as a value to get their job done. Another might have to have "high autonomy" to get their job done, and too much connection might hamper them. Some might need "innovation" and "risk tolerance." Others might need "security" and "high-risk management." That is why I talk about getting specific to finding out what values and behaviors actually drive the results you are looking to produce.

Make Specific Covenants for Behaviors

A covenant is a promise to perform. I like to see teams come together and make covenants to behave in certain ways, similar to the list of values I shared above. If you go back and read the language there, they listed active verbs that showed clearly how they covenant to behave with one another. When they fulfill those covenants, their values will be realized and their objectives met. Here are a few of their behaviors they promise to deliver to one another:

> We partner with our colleagues to achieve results.
>
> We intentionally build strong collaborative relationships with our customers.
>
> We set clear, strategically aligned goals and focus on execution of priorities while balancing short-term and long-term business needs.
>
> We listen to understand and respectfully question to achieve clarity.
>
> Get with your team and figure out what the covenants are that are going to make your values realized, and which will drive your results.

Develop Accountability Systems

As I mentioned before, great teams are driven by performance. And several things fuel performance, but two of the most important ingredients are measurement and accountability. So teams must ask themselves and agree upon: How will they measure how well they are "behaving"? How will they hold each other accountable for what they have agreed to do? For their values? How will they know that they are getting there? How will they hold each other accountable for the drivers that will get them to the goal? What are the benchmarks? How will they define results?

As we have talked about, it is not good enough to just measure results and let that be the metric that is watched. It is important, but it is only the outcome, not the real driver. The score of the football game is the result, but the number of fumbles, interceptions, and penalties are the *driver metrics.* Those are the behaviors that drive the result. Sales may be the score, but number of presentations before qualified leads is a driver. As mentioned before, figure out the right metrics for the team members to contribute to what you have decided to do together, and then hold each other accountable for those drivers. And through trust, help each other in the places where you are falling behind or struggling. Make it OK to confess to the team that you are not getting it done and ask for help.

Put In an Observing Structure

One of the most powerful practices a team can use is to "observe themselves." We know why this works in the operational arenas, as teams regularly look at their numbers and their performance and make adjustments. But what I am talking about is a different kind of observation. *It is the practice of the team observing "how it is working."*

Once you establish the team values and behaviors, or the elements that are going to build trust, or the covenants, do a few things to help you observe yourself to see how you are executing the values themselves. Observe yourself living out the values, not just observing and counting the number of widgets you are selling.

How? Very simple: First, take about five or ten minutes at the end of your regular team meetings and ask the question "How did we do today on practicing our values?" Observe how well you did what you said you were going to do. Did you "get the dead fish out of the drawer"? Did you "communicate to understand"? Did you achieve "connectedness" of the parts? How could you do better? Whatever you have decided your values are, ask yourself how you did today?

Second, appoint someone for each meeting to be in charge of sharing how he or she is living out that value in the teams that they lead below them. Or have that person bring in an example of where she sees it working in day-to-day endeavors. Or have him share an article or news story that illustrates a team value. The point is for the team to be invested in helping each other get better in executing the values, and also to keep the values in front of them on an ongoing basis. Working memory.

Third, make time and space to work on building the team. I cannot stress this enough. The best companies take time to get away, find a good facilitator to help them, and are diligent about building their teams. It is a discipline, and they spend time and money on doing it. They do not just assume that it is going to happen. If you just assume it, what you will get is a team falling into default patterns and paralysis.

But if you invest the time and energy, you will reap the results.

QUESTIONS TO ASK

What is the current level of trust on your team?

What do you need to do to work on trust, to define it, and to understand one another around trust?

Using the definition and elements listed above, how would you say your team is doing on connection through understanding, motivation and intent, character, capacity and ability, and track record in relation to their ability to trust one another?

CHAPTER 10

BOUNDARIES FOR YOURSELF

There is a law of leadership physics that affects many leaders without their being aware of it, and it can do them in if they are not careful. But if they are, they can soar. The law is this: the higher you go in leadership, the fewer external forces act upon you and dictate your focus, energy, and direction. Instead you set the terms of engagement and direct your own path, with only the reality of results to push against you.

For example, if you work the counter in a retail chain, the definition of what you do and the direction of your efforts has pretty well been defined. The forces have acted upon you. Obviously there are specific behaviors a checkout clerk controls that can add significantly to the bottom line and are extremely important, but the fundamental activities of the job have already been defined. By contrast, although a CEO has a board of directors that usually sets policy guidelines, targets, and so forth, she is nevertheless in control of determining how the organization will achieve the desired results. Most of the "how" is up to her, and she will be held accountable for the results she brings about.

So since your direction depends much upon you, and with so much hanging in the balance, there's a question that becomes very important to answer: *How are you leading yourself?*

Here is the physics problem in a nutshell. Too many times leaders, in the absence of someone looking over their shoulder, allow the reality of the mission or the circumstances to lead and to shape them. They get into a reactive mode, always responding to external forces and problems, and quickly losing sight of their larger role and purpose. The crush of urgent crises, to-do lists, squeaky wheel people, and distracting details takes over. It can feel very much like it is a war "out there" that requires shooting and ducking every waking hour of every day. *In this flurry of activity, too many leaders forget that they also need to manage themselves, since no one else is doing it*; they fail to put into place key boundaries of *self*-leadership that the sheer volume of work and responsibilities can obscure.

No one else can set these boundaries for you. All great leaders know, or come to recognize, that they must do it for themselves—that is, if they want to be the kind of leaders who sustain themselves over the course of many years and through all sorts of change and upheaval. Let's look at some of those self-boundaries.

LEADERS OPEN THEMSELVES TO OUTSIDE INPUTS

The Second Law of Thermodynamics says that everything in the universe is running down, running out of energy, and becoming less organized and more disordered. (Gee, does this sound like any businesses you know?)

But an important aspect of that law is that it only applies to a closed system, meaning that it applies to things that are left unto themselves and shut off from outside intervention. You have seen this if you have young kids. Leave them in charge for a weekend and see if the house is more or less orderly when you return, if they are a closed system left unto themselves.

But in an open system, the result is quite different. Disorder and decline are not inevitable and can, in fact, be reversed if the system opens itself up to two things: a new source of *energy* and a *template* (a template is anything that serves as a guide, pattern, or model). You need *force* and you need the *intelligence to inform action*. If you have those two things, higher order functioning can take place. In a very tangible way, that is what leaders do when they pump *energy* and *guidance* into an organization or a team.

But what about the leader herself? Remember, she is a system too, subject to running down and getting more disordered and off track, *left unto herself.* Conversely, if she opens up to outside sources of energy and intelligence, she can get better and better. This brings us to the first self-boundary:

Set a boundary on your tendency to be a "closed system," and open yourself to outside inputs that bring you energy and guidance.

I recently had a conversation with a friend of mine, one of those genius types who holds patents on three or four inventions, including one that he'd successfully launched as a very successful commercial product. His little project had turned into a growing company almost overnight, and suddenly he was confronted with all sorts of questions outside of his core skill set. Questions about financing debt, outsourcing manufacturing, overseas expansion, branding, and packaging—all very important, but not areas where Scott was at his best. He was upset when several of his board members suggested that he get some help from outside experts in these specialized areas. That made him nervous, since he was so accustomed to being the smartest guy in the room. But what upset him even more was their suggestion that he also start working with an executive coach to help him hone his "people skills." They made it clear that they thought he needed to step up his game as a leader, and not just keep being a brilliant tinkerer in the garage. Scott was annoyed and anxious when we started talking.

As a leadership consultant, I am all too familiar with Scott's reaction. Like a lot of rookie leaders, Scott had worn his ability to handle almost everything that came his way as a point of pride—up until the point where his isolation became his Achilles heel. Seasoned champions, on the other hand, are well connected and bolstered with a strong support system, a personal advisory board, a coach, and plenty of mentors who inject new energy and resources into the mix. Great leaders simply don't buy the old saying that it is lonely at the top, even if they do accept that the buck stops with them. *When it does stop with you, the last thing you need to be is isolated.*

When I say "isolated" I'm talking about the unnecessary risks leaders take when they don't seek out any form of support or input and are shielded. And I would go further and say that leaders need more input and more support than the kind that is available inside the organization or from the board of directors. Most leaders have a mentor or a boss inside the company who acts as an important sounding board, but that is still a "closed system." What I'm talking about is *outside* support and input—support from people who can be objective, who don't have a vested interest in outcomes, other than their care for the leader and his personal and professional growth. That should be their one interest—wanting to help the leader do well for himself and for whomever his stakeholders are. Sometimes these inputs are needed to help a leader refuel or develop, stay motivated, get through a valley, or overcome obstacles. Sometimes they are needed to protect the leader from his own worst instincts. At other times, they provide new ways of doing things in the business or new models of leading for a particular circumstance. Leaders need outside voices to provide emotional and functional support, not just so they can avoid mistakes but also so they can grow as leaders.

I had a client once who received a scathing and scolding e-mail from the chairman of the board on a Friday morning; it was full of erroneous conclusions and unchecked accusations, stemming from some personal friction the two had experienced in the past. Sadly, it wasn't the first time this had happened, and my client had finally had enough. He put together a response that meticulously dismantled each of the chairman's points, revealing how far from reality the criticism had been. His tone was calm and clinical, but his intellectual condemnation of the chairman was brutal. It was as if the captain of the debate team had just crushed the competition. Just before he hit the "send" button with a "cc" to the rest of the members of the board, he decided to call me.

"I sent you my response to Aaron's e-mail, and I thought before I sent it to him and the board, I would see if you had any additional input," he said.

"OK," I said. "I will take a look and call you right back."

Then I read his e-mail and was shocked. Ouch. It was a scorcher. If he had wanted to totally and publicly humiliate someone, in a "non-angry" way, this was the way to do it. But he would be winning the battle while losing the war.

I called him back. "OK, sit down and listen. Here is what you do. Go home, go for a swim, watch a movie, and have a nice weekend. Read through the e-mail again on Monday and then call me. But whatever you do, *don't send it*," I said.

"Why?" he asked.

"Because I know you, and it will accomplish nothing that you want to accomplish, and will do very destructive things that you don't want," I said.

"Really? Is it that bad?" he asked.

"No," I said. "It is worse. But put it aside for now and call me next week."

Later, the next week, we talked about it, and he could see what had happened. He could see how in his "fact-driven way" he was totally out of control and had let his anger drive the agenda. It would accomplish little of what he really wanted. In the rush of emotion, he had forgotten his own boundaries, spun out of control, and failed to keep his larger goals in mind. He could see that now, but it had taken "outside eyes" (mine) to look at the situation and to give him the objective feedback that he needed—feedback that he could not provide for himself in such an angry state.

The fact is that we all get subjective and do not see the whole truth, about ourselves or about others. We need outside eyes to help us. We need another set of ears to hear what is going on. To not recognize that is the height of arrogance. If you have not set boundaries to prevent yourself from being an isolated leader, then all you have is your own eyes and ears to rely on. Or perhaps you can call upon someone within your closed system, that tiny universe made up of so-called advisers who sometimes want nothing more than to further their own agendas. And in doing that, they often won't be honest with you.

I recently was referred to a CEO by another CEO who told him, "One of the reasons he will be most helpful to you is that he [meaning me] does not need you. He does not need your business or need to please you in any way. Therefore, he will tell you the truth, whereas someone else might be afraid to do that." That is one of the values of outside input. Their voices aren't muffled by conflicts of interest that may be present when you consult the internal advisers you already have. While internal advisers are essential, outside ones are different. They protect you by having no conflict of interest; they are only there to help you, not to serve themselves, if they are good ones.

LEADERS IDENTIFY WHERE THEY NEED FRESH INPUT

Another reason to become an open system is because you might be facing something you never have faced before. I got a call for a consulting project where the CEO said, "I need help to change the culture in this organization. The culture that I have inherited is never going to be able to pull off the vision I have going forward. We have to have a new one, and I know exactly what it has to be," he said. "I can send it to you and then we can talk."

He sent me the document, and I was very impressed. He had thought through the culture change very strategically and with laserlike accuracy. The alignment of what the culture needed with the drivers of the vision was already rock star quality. But when I called him back, his *open-system thinking was easily seen.*

"I read your document," I said. "It seems like you know what you need to do, so what do you need me for?" I asked.

"I know what I need to do," he said. "I just don't know how to do it. I have never taken an organization through a culture change before, and I need someone walking with me who has done it, and showing me how to pull that off."

I knew that I was going to love this client and this project. He knew where he needed new input, *not because he was not a seasoned leader, but because he found himself in a situation that he had not encountered before and was looking outside of himself to get input.* The more I came to know him, and saw the level at which he thought, I could see how he had become so successful. He had never been limited by his own thinking, and had always turned to trusted advisers when he needed to get better. And he always had gotten better over time. *He had opened the system to grow it.*

Being an open system means, basically, that you are not arrogant enough to think that you have all the answers, or that your organization has all the answers, or even that you should. You know that there is experience and energy outside of what you bring that can add to your personal and organizational infrastructure, and you open yourself up to it. In my experience, when there is a real problem in an organization at the top, one of the issues always in the picture is a leader who cannot take objective input or who is arrogant. They have corporate boards comprised of "yes" people, and they surround themselves with others who do not tell them the truth out of fear. Or there are those who do tell them the truth and are marginalized.

So, think about this question: How much do you open up to

outside sources of information, feedback, support, energy, expertise, etc.? Your answer might reveal why you feel stuck and why the laws of physics have been working against you. The closed system you've created is winding down and getting messier. So what can you do?

My advice is to plug in to sources outside of yourself and your organization. Get coaching, join a leadership group or forum, avail yourself of continuing education, attend a leadership conference, and so forth. The best leaders and organizations I know make use of outside sources for coaching and lifelong learning in a very organic fashion. One of my client companies, for example, regularly sends its upper level leaders to experiences like Harvard Business School's executive programs. They also require and fund outside leadership coaches for their executives. Open system change is integral to their culture, and you can see it working. They are growing every year—not just their business, but the leadership talent as well. And that is what is driving the business growth.

The physics are clear: close down, and get worse. Or, open up and get better.

LEADERS ARE HUNGRY FOR FEEDBACK

Ken Blanchard says that feedback is the "breakfast of champions." There is no doubt about that, as learning how we are doing and how to do better are key to any performance. In fact, the best performance situations are when we are getting the most immediate feedback, which is from the task itself, as flow researcher Mihaly Csikszentmihalyi has found.

The problem tends to occur at that moment when we actually get the feedback, either from other people or from the outcomes themselves. That is when our leadership character shows itself. While Blanchard gets it exactly right about the kind of breakfast we need, the truth is that *not everyone has the same appetite for breakfast*. Some people wake up and really want it, while it makes others sick to their stomachs. Some are *allergic* to feedback.

Brain research shows that feedback can do funny things to us if we see it as a danger or a put-down. We go into the "moving away" or "moving against" mode of fight-or-flight. The brain gets biochemically goofy. That is why you see people get so defensive and go to great lengths to fight any feedback. *But remember, fight-or-flight only comes when there is a perceived danger.* Therein is the rub. If we see feedback as dangerous, we will bristle and fight it. But if we perceive feedback as an unexpected windfall, like winning the lottery, we will seek it out and be open to it, and sometimes even pay for it. That is what good character does . . . it *hungers* for feedback.

To be the best you can be, you must develop a hunger for feedback and see it as one of the best gifts that you can get. It is part of being an open system and has incredible value not only to you but also to your people.

I was conducting a leadership offsite where the executive team members responsible for the agenda had asked me to try to maneuver the conversation toward a topic they all wanted to discuss but didn't want to state explicitly on the agenda. After a lot of discussion about why I had to "maneuver" it that way instead of just intentionally designing it that way, the team confessed that their real goal was to sneak some tough feedback about the CEO onto the agenda—but in a way that would not throw him off or make him defensive. They feared that if the agenda were openly designed to give him feedback, it would never work. They hoped I would be able to "go there if the mood was right." How sneaky, a lot of pressure, and not a lot of hope for success, I thought. I told them I understood their concerns but that I had a different plan for how to get the CEO into the right zone.

So at the beginning of the meeting, I explained the "physics of leadership" and the importance of the Second Law of Thermodynamics, mentioned above. I explained why it is important for senior leaders to be an open system and model receiving feedback well in organizations, and I emphasized that being open to feedback is a key indicator not only of leadership aptitude but also of character. Good character welcomes feedback and foolish character fights it off. (See my book *Necessary Endings* for more on how wise people desire feedback and foolish people fight it.)

I don't know whether it was these comments or the mood—or whether the team had just misread the CEO—but when the time came for "saying things that are hard to say, but necessary for the good of the vision," one of the members of the executive team had the courage to wade in. He told the CEO that there were some things that they needed from him that they were not getting, and that there were some things in his leadership style that was leaving the team and the organization with some gaps in performance. I watched and held my breath, waiting for the whole retreat to blow up before my eyes. (I love those moments, though. They can be some of the most powerful.)

The CEO listened as this tough feedback came at him in front of his whole team. And he did what the great leaders do: *He received it, and he thanked them for it.*

They looked stunned. But what was amazing was the discussion that followed. The CEO talked about his own passions, and the strengths and weaknesses that made him lead that way. His candor broke the logjam, and the team was able to come together and offer ways to help the CEO deal with his challenges. What made it happen was the CEO's *receptivity to hearing what his stakeholders had to say—his willingness to embrace it and make changes.* And part of what made him receptive was hearing from me, an outsider, that it was more than okay—it was normal and even desirable—to hear and receive feedback. Now, four years later, the team still refers to that moment as "the retreat where we got honest." It was the beginning of a shift in the entire culture, ignited by the CEO's openness to feedback.

What is your appetite for feedback and receptivity to it? Do you get defensive, or reactive? To the extent that you see it as adversarial, your brain will fight it or move away from it. But if you can make receiving feedback part of your value system, if you can frame it as one of the best gifts that you can ever have, then you will become an open system for change. You will move toward it. You will seek it. You will even *pay* someone to give it to you. When you do that, there is no limit to how much you can grow.

Set very, very strong boundaries with yourself against any tendency you might have toward defensiveness, blame, or denial when given feedback. The weakest leaders are threatened by feedback, and often completely closed off to insights that are so easily seen by others. Strong leaders embrace feedback, seek to understand it, and put it to use. Even when they may disagree, they don't become defensive; instead they engage in dialogue and honest inquiry to figure out where the gaps between their intentions and others' perceptions come from. The feedback may be wrong, but they embrace it to understand it nevertheless. You can embrace and not agree at the same time. Move toward it.

BOUNDARIES ON THINKING AND FEARS

I have not met a leader who thinks perfectly rationally 100 percent of the time. All humans have a tendency toward goofy or distorted interpretations of events and other people's motives, especially under extreme stress. And all of us have our insecurities, and those touchy buttons that, when pushed, cause our thinking to go awry and our fears to be magnified.

The key is to know your own particular style of kookiness. Once you know your own patterns, you can recognize them and change them. While there is no limit to the variations on distorted thinking that affect performance, there are some patterns that crop up more often than not. These include: overidentification with results, indecisiveness, conflict avoidance, and resistance to change. Let me explain.

DON'T DEFINE YOURSELF BY OUTCOMES

One of the most performance-limiting and devastating ways of thinking is to overidentify with a particular result. In other words, less-than-great leaders often evaluate themselves in terms of a particular outcome, and allow it to define who they are and what they can do. They look to the latest quarter's results, or their balance sheet, a boss's or board's approval, or some other arbitrary measure to tell them if they are "good enough." By contrast, *the greatest leaders embrace outcomes, and own them, but they do not let them define who they are.* They learn from them. If Eli Manning throws an interception, he doesn't all of a sudden think of himself as a "loser" and allow the three P's to take over. He watches the films of the game and learns from his mistakes. He is not the interception. He is Eli who threw an interception. Big difference. So Eli, the great quarterback, learns from the interception and throws a touchdown on the next attempt.

Set boundaries on your tendency to allow single events or results to define you. You are not your last bad result. Look to more dependable measures, and hold yourself to better standards than any single outcome. Ask if you are performing to your defined values, behaviors, and activities, and forget about keeping track of the daily score. Instead evaluate whether your process is still aligned with the specific behaviors and activities that are going to drive big-picture results. *Evaluate yourself using the real drivers of ultimate results.* Look for improvement along those significant measures, not perfection or immediate wins. No leader is immune to losses, bad quarters, bad years, bad reviews, or product failures. It is part of the game, and part of getting it right. What matters is how you learn from these challenges and use them to improve. Focus on the things that are going to drive improvement. *Do not let any one loss tell you who you are or what your potential or future is.* If you do, your brain functioning will be changed and you will perform at a lower level.

Earlier when we talked about the three P's, we were looking at making sure your people were not infected with learned helplessness thinking patterns. But remember, you can be subject to the same disease. Ask yourself these questions:

Personalizing: What event or other person has made you begin to question yourself and your capabilities? What or who has the power to make you go negative? What outcome have you been personalizing to your detriment?

Pervasive: What outcome or person has had the power to make you begin to feel bad about more than that one event or outcome, that is, you begin to feel like everything is going south? You begin to question the company, the industry, or more?

Permanent: What outcome or person has had the ability for you to feel like it is never going to be good? What is making you see the future negatively?

Remember the first person you have to lead is *yourself*, and if someone or any outcome has that much power over you, you have lost your rudder. Get it back by putting some very firm boundaries around the power that you have handed over to others to have that kind of control over you. Implement the program that I described in chapter 6 for yourself, and open yourself up to people who can be objective. Even the best leaders can sometimes fall victim to negative periods. If it happens to you, don't think you are weird. Just recognize it for what it is, get back in control of your thinking, and open up to some help.

DON'T BE RULED BY FEAR

"I know that I hold on to people too long, way past when I know I have to make a change," a CEO told me. "I have always done that, and it costs me."

"What are you afraid of?" I asked.

"I don't think I am afraid," he said. "I just don't want to hurt them and I always try to protect them."

"What's the fear?" I asked again.

It took him a while to get to it, but underneath it all, he was afraid for others to have to go through a struggle.

"So, have you ever been told you were not doing well and had to learn to do better?" I asked.

"Of course," he said. "More than once."

"What was the outcome? Did it kill you?" I asked.

"Actually, those were some of the most valuable times that got me here," he said.

"So why are you afraid to give that gift to someone else when they need it? Let it do its work," I argued.

He got it but had to examine the fear that was holding him back before he could see it clearly.

The problem is that the brain is wired to avoid pain and anxiety. Over time, when you continue to avoid things that cause you fear or anxiety, such as this CEO's fear of letting someone struggle, a pattern builds up, causing you to respond almost automatically to any situations that would cause you that anxiety. As a leader, you cannot allow a pattern of fear and avoidance to rule you. If you are afraid of making a mistake, you will never make bold moves. If you are afraid of upsetting or disappointing people, you will never be able to deal with underperforming employees. As a leader, you have to act (or not act), despite the fear but never *because* of it.

In my experience, many great leaders go through a three-stage process when it comes to facing their fears. First, they fear it and put it off. Next, they push through the fear, make the decision, and it is painful. And finally, *they wonder why they waited so long to make it after the pain is gone and they have resolved the problem.* As these stages are internalized, and they become aware of them, seasoned leaders find it easier to make these hard calls. But as long as you don't confront those uncomfortable feelings, your emotions will control your actions. Grow past the fear! Look at what you are afraid of and get to the bottom of it. Is it failure? Is it loss of approval? Is it fear of confrontation? Is it fear of causing someone distress? Is it fear of change? And remember: You can have fears without being "fearful." "Fearful" is when you let your fears make your decisions for you, so . . . don't let fear make your decisions for you! Having fears is normal. Being "fearful" is dysfunctional. *Fearful leaders—that is, those who respond out of fear—are the worst leaders, period.*

So, feel your fear, name it, accept it, talk it over with those you trust, and then choose to do the right thing, *no matter how uncomfortable you feel.* People are waiting on you! Lead! Who cares how you feel?! Do what is needed and work through the feelings later.

DON'T PUT OFF CHANGE

One of the most important self-boundaries that leaders have to establish is against the tendency to put off changes that they know need to be made. If you think about it, much "waiting" and putting off changes has nothing to do with "getting more information," or "waiting until we get finished with *a*, *b*, or *c*." Obviously, it's essential to gather data and do analysis, but many leaders allow too much lag time between *knowing* and *doing*. Relocations, changing personnel, restructures, making significant investments, dropping vendors or other alliances, IT makeovers, shutting down a brand or strategy, selling or closing a business unit or department—changes like this tend to be very disruptive. But so was the American Revolution and the Civil War, and things were better as a result. It takes leadership to pull the trigger. Your mission is waiting on you.

I remember once when I had a decision to make regarding a significant investment. I had been reluctant to green light the deal because it was in an area that I was less familiar with than I wanted to be. The truth, however, was that my advisers were experts in this arena, and I really did trust their opinions. Still, I was putting it off. Finally one of them, the lead investor, called me.

"We have to go forward now or it is not going to happen," he said. "What are you going to do?"

"I want to talk to David first about some more balance sheet issues, and then I will let you know," I said.

"What *specific* information do you still need that will help you make the decision?" he asked. "What *exactly* do you need to know to go ahead? And what are you going to learn that you don't already know?"

When he put it that way, I realized something. *There was no more piece of specific information that I needed.* I was just looking for more comfort and there was *no info that was ever going to give me that.* I had to decide, to trust the smart people, and to eat my discomfort. I had to pull the trigger.

"You are right," I said. "There is nothing I am going to learn that will materially change anything. I am waiting, but I guess I am not waiting on any 'thing.' Let's do it. I will get the money wired today."

Look out for this dynamic in yourself by asking: What's holding me back? Is it lack of information or fear of making a mistake? Put some boundaries around the "need for more information" and the desire for absolute certainty. With most big decisions, risk cannot be entirely eliminated. Deal with it and get moving.

Another resistance to change is the desire to "make sure everyone is on board," or "we reach consensus," which is sometimes code for "I want to make sure everyone is going to like it." Just as it's essential to get good information, it's also important to align key people around the proposed change. At the same time, getting absolutely everyone on board may take forever, and making everyone happy with your decision is highly unlikely anyhow. Sometimes, after everyone has been heard and understood and has been able to have their input considered, you might have to make a decision that all are not happy with. That too is leadership. Sometimes you may even have to ask your team to "disagree but commit." But you cannot wait around for everyone to get happy, which leads to yet another key boundary that leaders must address: boundaries with the forces that resist change.

Resistance to change is a fact of life. If you want change to take hold, you *must* have good boundaries to contain the forces that are working against the effort. Typically change initiatives are confronted by three types of reactions, as explained by change expert John Kotter. One group will "get it" and be on board with you. Your role is to enlist them in your effort, deploying them to exercise influence with potential allies and to communicate positive messages about the change. The second group is the skeptics, who will not be so quick to come on board. With skeptics, their concerns are often legitimate and well intentioned, so you must engage them and address their issues. They *are* movable, if you do not allow their skepticism to become the leading narrative. Embrace them and bring them along, step by step. The third group is composed of the "no-no's," who are dead set against the change and unlikely to be persuaded otherwise. They require a different boundary altogether. As Kotter points out in his book, *A Sense of Urgency*, ignoring them is not an option, but there are a few ways you can effectively deal with them: distract them (give them something else to do so their energy and attention are elsewhere); expose them (keep them in the light so their arguments are seen by all to be just negativity and resistance); or remove them. *But you have to set boundaries that prevent them from influencing others.* The degree to which you allow the naysayers to take root will be the degree to which your change initiative fails. They can truly kill it, and you must set boundaries that will not allow that to take place.

BOUNDARIES ON BEING DISENGAGED WITH STAKEHOLDERS

Earlier we discussed the need for outside feedback, but there is another group that you must be very diligent about seeking feedback from: *your key stakeholders*. These are the people and the groups that have a vested interest in your performance. How you are doing with them really matters. So an important leadership boundary is to strategically plan the amount of time and distance you allow between critical touch points with these folks.

Leaders who don't set these boundaries end up paying for it. I've seen that happen far too often. While it isn't the only source of feedback, *it is nevertheless critical that you always have a good feel and a strong sense for how you are doing with those who have a stake in your performance and your organization's results*. I'm talking about members of your team, your board of directors, your investors, key customers and suppliers, strategic partners, government entities, and so forth. Most are good people, but remember, just because you are not paranoid doesn't mean that others are not out to get you.

See these touch points as a dashboard, telling you how you are doing at meeting the needs and expectations of these key constituents. Part of building and monitoring a performance culture within the organization is achieved by building a track record of setting and meeting expectations. To do that, it is critical that you are hearing from the ones that matter, understanding the things that matter to *them* that you provide, and determining their level of satisfaction with your performance. You also need to know what they need from you in order to satisfy their own stakeholders as well. Help them win with those who matter to them. How well they do sometimes depends on your performance; being able to help them win with their constituents is an important leadership skill as well. Tending to this boundary will prevent stakeholders from drifting away toward disengagement or, worse yet, gathering up other forces to move against you.

I recently got a call from the CEO of an organization on whose board I serve. He suggested lunch. I didn't know what the agenda was until I got there, but I assumed he might want to discuss some strategy or initiative or something like that. But when we sat down, he said, "So, I just wanted to get together to see how you as a board member think everything is going, how I am doing, any way I could serve the board better, or whatever other input you have for me."

While I am always careful with conversations outside the regular board context, and would usually not say anything that the rest of the board would not be privy to, this was not one of those weird conversations. This was true desire on his part to serve his board well, as key stakeholders in his performance. He was making the rounds with all of us, soliciting our thoughts about how we thought everything was going. Gathering our feedback, he suggested, would help him shape some directions for the board to formally discuss together, and improve his performance. I admired his approach: it had no "political" or manipulative feel to it—just a hunger to serve his board well.

As Bob Dylan said, "You gotta serve somebody." That is always true, and being diligent about staying in touch with whom you serve, and those really affected by your performance, is fundamental to your effectiveness. But where your heart is, and your motivation is, is everything in this point. You never, ever, want to be seen as a political maneuverer, someone who manages up and around by creating side alliances and trying to become close to influencers for political gain. Nothing is worse in an organization than a political operator who tries to curry favor with power bases, either above or below, for personal advancement. It is divisive, and you can smell that a mile away. *The process of staying in touch, whether with those above you, below you, around you, outside the organization, or the customers, should always be in the spirit of service.* It should be done to find out how you can serve them better, what they need from you, and what you need from them to serve the mission itself. It is never about self-advancement but about seeking to meet their needs. "How can I best meet your needs?" is a question that every stakeholder wants to hear. If you do that, you will never have to worry about advancing.

BOUNDARIES ON YOUR WEAKNESSES

I worked with a CEO who was one of the smartest people I have ever seen. He could look at a market landscape, a competitive environment, or a product offering and instantly see the value, the end game, in a flash. And most of the time he was right. The problem was that his massive strategic intelligence did not always translate into good leadership. He often left his team in the dust, utterly confused. It was as if he had just completed a complicated calculus problem by blurting out the answer without showing the work or the thinking that had gotten him there.

"We just need him to connect the dots a little bit," one VP said. "If he would do that, we could take it from there. But he comes back to us frustrated at times that we are still back at step one wondering how he thinks we are actually going to get there. He might be Houdini, but we need a key to the padlock."

So, what to do? The last thing we wanted was to put the brakes on his brain's processing power. It had been worth billions in revenues. Don't slow that one down. But we did need to put some boundaries around his weak communications skills. He had to become aware of how his strength in one area led to a weakness in another and make sure that he limited the problems and confusion that could cause.

He began with recognizing it as true. I got him to listen to the feedback from the team, so he could not just write them off individually as "not getting it," as he had done in the past. As the old saying goes, if one person calls you a horse, blow it off. But if five do, buy a saddle. When he heard it from the whole team, he had to listen, and he did. Before I got him to do that, though, he had always walked around scratching his head, wondering "what's wrong with those people." Back to open system change, it took an outsider to validate their complaints and get him to hear. So he had to wonder, "What's wrong with me?"

"Finally," they all felt.

Second, we made a team covenant that if anyone was not "getting it" at any moment, it would be seen as a *gift to the team* if they interrupted and just said, "I don't see how you got from here to there. Show us the steps." Whereas before they feared being seen as "slow," now his team members could become heroes for announcing their confusion publicly. At times when someone would do that, someone else would inevitably say "thank you, I was wondering the same thing." Others laughed, feeling the same way. It became fun.

Third, we identified someone on the team to act as a kind of

COO of team communications. This person was in charge of filling in the gaps between the CEO's pronouncements and the action steps required to bring his ideas into reality. The effect was twofold: it kept the group from walking out the door with misunderstandings still lingering, and it brought them closer together, as the "translator" clarified for the CEO what additional information and direction he needed to provide to his team. Once the CEO stepped into the gap caused by his weakness, everything got better. But he had to put a boundary around it, limit its effect, and not let it continue to rule the group.

Another CEO I know who is a great deal maker had to build a firewall that prevented him from touching anything in operations. If he messed with operations, chaos ensued. But, wow, could he do deals! He put a boundary on his weakness, and let his strength soar. Another leader I worked with was prone to overspending the company's resources on new deals, so he had to put a boundary around his tendency to do that with a new form of governance. The board loved it, and he was free to use his gifts, now that they couldn't get the company into trouble.

BOUNDARIES WITH YOUR TIME AND ENERGY

One of my favorite practices is a time audit. This is a no excuses, no blame, take-ownership exercise that can be used by anyone to identify gaps between stated priorities and time and effort spent. In other words, if you say that the most important thing in your leadership is to open new markets, and yet when you audit your time, you have spent only 10 percent of your time doing that, you have caught yourself in the crime. The higher you go as a leader, the more responsible for yourself you are for how you allocate your time. The higher you go, the less you have someone looking over your shoulder The cookie jar is yours. No blaming anyone else.

Unfortunately I've seen too many leaders who don't act like they are in charge of their time, even though they truly are.

So, do the audit. When you find that the clear priorities that you have set for yourself are not getting the best of your time and energy, ask yourself why. Where are the leaks? Who are you having difficulty saying no to? Is it a lack of planning? Whose crises are you always solving or whose work are you doing instead of your own? Who is the squeaky wheel getting all of your attention? Set some boundaries.

And remember the "big rocks first" rule. If you put the big rocks in a jar first, you can also get the little rocks in, then the sand, and then the water. But if you do the smaller stuff first, the big rocks will never fit. Your time is like that. What is vital to achieve your vision? Are those getting on the schedule first? Give them first priority, but *assign them a time and place, so that they actually get done.*

If you do not give them a time and place in the calendar, they will get pushed out because of yet another urgent crisis. For example, in my coaching work with CEOs and other executives, we will schedule the times we will be together months in advance. Since they have seen that time as vital, they have to get it in the calendar before the urgent stuff gets in the way. The same holds true for the work we will do with their executive team, such as quarterly offsites. Those are big rocks that will come first. *CEOs tell me that the discipline of the quarterly offsite meetings is one of the most important structures that they have, once we have done it for a while.* It makes certain that the vital work gets done. Once they see its benefits they don't let it slide. In my work, I have always seen a high correlation between success and the leader's propensity to put the vital activities, such as team building or strategic work, in the calendar first and not move it later. They have the discipline to do what is vital but not "urgent."

So, what are your "big rocks"?

What is "vital" that you should put in the schedule first?

My work, for example, consists of four big chunks or categories. First is the time I spend consulting and coaching leaders and their teams. That is what I call the "real stuff," as it is the essence of all that I do. It is my heart as a practitioner, and without it, I would have nothing meaningful to say. But in doing that work, I tend to recognize principles and constructs, thereby creating a lot of intellectual property and content. I put all of that content together in the form of workshops, training programs, and books like the one you are reading now. Much of my business is about creating programs for companies that build their leaders, teams, cultures, and performance.

Third, I deliver that content about leadership, business, and performance by giving speeches at conferences and working with various media to disseminate core principles and insights. Finally, there are the executive tasks of "running the business"—operations, booking events, and other administrative and operational needs.

So I know that to make it all work, each category has to have its due. And if I don't plan accordingly, if I don't put the big rocks in first, the urgent will push the vital out of the picture. So I have to set aside a certain number of days or weeks for content creation, for writing books, or for training and development programs for organizations. And I have a limited budget of available consulting or coaching days per year, so I have to guard them for my clients and choose my clients well to decide with whom I want to spend those days. That boundary of having only so many available days forces other good disciplines, like which clients to say yes or no to, knowing that I only have so many slots to offer. It also forces the discipline to plan well to make sure I have days available for content creation and delivery in the other categories.

The lesson is this: boundaries on time, just like financial budgets, *force us to prioritize good decisions.* If we treat time like it is unlimited, we will say yes to a lot of things that really are not high value. And we lose our way. When you know how much time you have available, and that it is fixed, you will spend it strategically. It forces you to focus on what truly drives the business. So, in my audit, I have to make sure that I have allocated the right number of days for the strategic drivers I want to accomplish in any given period. If I don't, none of them gets the right kind of attention or focus. Recently I had the executive assistant to the CEO of a $25 billion company ask me, "Can you help him learn how to say no to people? He promises more time to people than he has, and I have to be the one who says no later. He just does not get it that there is only so much time available and if he says yes to something, that means no to something else." Well said.

I have found that when leaders begin to answer these questions of where they are going to budget time, they also uncover other issues that they didn't realize were holding them back. For instance, they find that a good percentage of their time goes to someone who is not doing his job, and then it becomes clear that it is time for a coaching or disciplinary session with that person. Or, they find that they really are doing the same thing over and over again, a task that should be delegated.

Do the audit regularly and use it to let you know where your leaks are and who is getting the best of you. I have seen this exercise result in hiring someone new, when a leader finds that he or she is doing a lot of activities that someone else could do if they would just create that position and hire that person. And I have seen it result in firing someone who, if they were doing their job, the leader would not have been doing it for them. And I have seen it result in reaching strategic objectives, now that a boundary has been set around the urgent, but not vital, activities that had sucked up time in the past.

Energy is a separate matter. Your energy is one of your biggest assets and must be managed. Figure out who and what drains yours. For example, if you have to do a key presentation or a negotiation that is crucial to your vision, do not schedule anything right before that will drain you. Schedule low-risk, low-intensity matters for those times when your energy may be ebbing, and save the vital work for times when your energy levels are highest. For example, when I write books, I need uninterrupted chunks of time to get in the flow. And writing time cannot be time that will come *after* something that is going to be a brain drain. I know what drains my energy, and I avoid scheduling these activities around times when I need to be most creative.

Another example is a conference call in a high-conflict situation. In my consulting work, I often find myself in emotionally intense meetings, either in person or on the phone, where I am in the position of helping others manage, negotiate, and resolve conflicts. These meetings require a lot of energy, a lot of focus, and often careful intervention on my part, sometimes when people are very angry or otherwise acting pretty kooky. After one of these sessions, I usually am not in the best frame of mind to think creatively. So at those times, I either do my own root canal or binge on salt-and-vinegar potato chips, but plan nothing creative that requires more than a lizard's brain.

And then there are people who are the *known* root canals that you have to regularly deal with as well. Some are unavoidable, but they still are draining. Make sure that you schedule those calls and meetings in spaces where you do not have to do anything afterward that requires any energy. Brain research has shown that the higher-thinking functions actually take physical energy. Allow yourself time to refuel after you experience one of these episodes, just as if you had come back from a long run on a hot summer's day. Give your brain a rest.

BOUNDARIES ON PATTERNS

Most people can see and solve a problem. But leaders must get *above* the problems that are not being solved and see that there may be more than a problem going on. Instead of a "problem" there may be a "pattern," and *patterns are what will end up ruining your business.* There are two kinds of patterns that I want you to look at that might require some boundaries.

The first is a pattern masquerading as a problem—that is, a problem or a situation that keep happening over and over again is not a problem. It is a pattern. Patterns can be with people—like Joe, who always misses deadlines for getting financial reporting done in time for you to prepare for your meetings. Or Susie, who fails to deal with poorly performing employees year after year until the point where you have to step in. Or Steve, whom you've asked to focus on new acquisitions but has still not found any targets because he is too busy tracking this quarter's numbers. Or your team, which always seems to smile in agreement but then breaks down into cliques and factions that bring an initiative to its knees. These are not isolated problems that are getting solved—they are *patterns* that have to be addressed. Let's start with Joe.

"Joe, you know we have talked about this deadline problem before, like in February, March, and now April. We have discussed what it costs us, and you told me that you were going to address it and not miss another one. But here we are again, so I don't want to talk about the April deadline as if that were the problem.

"Missing this deadline is not the problem. The problem is that missing deadlines is more than a problem. It is a pattern with you. So I do not want to talk about it anymore, as that does not help. I want to have a different conversation. I want to talk about the fact that talking about problems with you does not help, and we need to do something different to stop the pattern. I cannot allow myself to be exposed to this problem in an ongoing way anymore."

From there, usually good things begin to happen, as you have broken through the denial. It is like crafting a New Year's resolution that you can actually live up to. "I have never lost weight thinking I will just get into shape next month. I need a program." More structure and consequences are usually needed, and if you address it as a pattern and require a more structured approach with some painful consequences, chances are that you will get somewhere. But otherwise, to ignore that there is a pattern is to participate in your own denial. It may be time that Joe gets some consequences to help him to deal with his pattern.*

But what if the pattern in question has to do with your own behavior? Recognizing the truth of that might be one of the best things you ever did for yourself. Your patterns will hold you back, unless you change them. Remember, it is not your gifts that will hold you back; *it is your patterns that get in the way of your gifts.*

By these patterns of weakness, I am not referring to areas where you do not have strengths or talents. Focusing on strengths and not weaknesses is important. For example, Michael Phelps should swim and not play golf. Bad golf is not a problematic pattern. We should always avoid the areas where we are not gifted and focus on our strengths instead. *I am referring to patterns that have to do with you as a person, such as being conflict-avoidant, or impulsive, or risk-adverse, or distracted, or overcommitted, or afraid of authority, or people pleasing, or resistant to making hard decisions, or fear of failure*, etc. Those are the kinds of patterns that have to do with your makeup and have to be addressed, as they will render your strengths unusable. We are not expected to have all the gifts or strengths. But we are expected to have sufficient emotional intelligence to be able to make our gifts profitable. Character is not negotiable. If Michael Phelps developed a pattern of avoiding cold water in the morning because he did not like the way it made him feel, and did not address that pattern, his gifts would never bring success. That is a weakness, not a lack of giftedness. There is a difference. Get over the fear of cold water so you can win some medals using your gifts.

---

* See the chapter "The Wise, the Foolish, and the Evil," in my book *Necessary Endings,* (New York: HarperCollins, 2011).

Just as when dealing with others, you have to break through your own denial. You have been telling yourself that you are going to do better, but it is not changing if it is still a pattern. *So it is time to add some structure and help from the outside.* Remember: open-system change. If you do that, then you can change it, but left unto yourself, you are more likely to keep repeating it.

Remember, you never need new ways to fail. The old ones are working just fine. And until they are addressed, they will continue to work.

At other times, these "problems that are patterns" involve the *business itself.* When your company totally misses a shift in the market, you can call that a mistake. Miss two or three in a row, and you can call it a pattern that *must* be addressed. If you don't, the board or the banks or the customers will address it for you.

Often problem patterns are as recognizable as TV characters. Watch out when you start hearing comments like this about your business: "They tend to be late to market." Or, "They tend to release something before it is ready, so I will wait for the next version." Leaders must be in the position to prevent these kinds of patterns from turning into a reputation—and a poor one at that. These patterns can begin to define the brand.

Here is the important distinction: problems, when addressed, are solved. Patterns, when addressed as if they were only a problem to be solved, remain. This is where many leaders get stuck, as they often are depending on someone's performance to turn around, yet it continues to be the same. They just keep telling them to do better. They only address the problem when they really ought to be addressing the underlying pattern. And sometimes even addressing the pattern won't change things. That's when the boundary of a "necessary ending" (as described in my book of the same name) may be required. A consequence is needed to break the pattern.

Then there is the second group of patterns, which is the *repetition of the same work*. What I mean by this is that if there is something that only you can do, at least in the beginning, *but then you find that you are doing that same thing over and over again in the same way, and you pretty much have it nailed, it might be time to turn that over to someone else.* There is a pattern of work, a repeatable formula, to what you are doing, and that means it is probably transferable. Leadership demands that you move it down the organizational tree. If there is a known path of the work, and it is repetitive, it can probably be taught. And if someone else can be taught to do it, it might be time to delegate that work, so that you can get back to doing what only you can do: lead.

At times, these repeatable patterns can even be pretty high-level activities, such as driving a merger or an acquisition. Sometimes, after you have done enough of those, the path is clear and the operational pattern for execution can be taught and handed over to someone else. Then you can reserve your time and effort for mergers or acquisitions (or whatever we are talking about) that are decidedly *different* or high stakes—and that *require the leader's deeper involvement.* Figure out what the business needs from you and only you, and do that.

STILL RIDICULOUSLY IN CHARGE

When you realize that you are ridiculously in charge, it does not only mean you are in charge of others or in charge of what goes on in the organization. It also means that you are ridiculously in charge of *yourself.* My experience with high-level leaders is that there are two kinds. The first kind of leader is defined by the work. The second kind is in a process of actively defining the work, and they do that by first defining themselves and taking charge of who they are going to be and how they are going to work. They have good self-leadership boundaries.

Think of it as another way of not just working in the business, but of working "on" the business by working on you. Lead with these boundaries on yourself, and you will be more in charge than you ever thought possible.

QUESTIONS TO ASK

How much do you lead yourself versus being led by outside forces?

How are you an open system? What do you need from the outside in terms of energy or a template?

In what areas do you need outside wisdom? Where can you get it?

Are you open to feedback? Where will you get it?

What thinking and fears do you need to set boundaries on?

Who are your key stakeholders and how do you keep in touch with how you are doing with them?

How will you protect yourself from your weaknesses?

How can you protect time and energy for when and how you need it? What big rocks need to be put in the schedule first?

What "patterns" are you treating as "problems" and need to treat differently?

CONCLUSION

My seatmate on a flight from California to Chicago was a retired CEO from the banking industry. We had been on a fun golfing trip and were just shooting the breeze. As we discussed leadership, he emphasized, "Leadership is everything." I asked him to explain, expecting him to tell me about how leaders create vision, strategy, and drive results. He would certainly know, as he had built a large and very successful banking enterprise from the ground up. He was an icon in the industry, recognized many times over for the company he had created. But that is not what he talked about.

What he talked about was the sad situation of a friend of his in another industry. He had also built a successful enterprise, creating great value for the stockholders and employees. Then he had retired and turned it over to someone else, who, according to my new friend, "drove it into the ground," destroying most of its value in the process.

"What did the new guy do wrong?" I asked.

"He did not focus on 'culture,'" he said.

As we talked more, he explained what he meant. The problem wasn't that the guy didn't have the right "plan," or the right amount of "smarts." The man knew the business, and had all the brains and business acumen necessary to get it done. In fact, as my friend described it, this guy had been chosen for that very reason, for how smart he was and for how well he knew the business. At the time, most people involved in the search process thought that he was "the best they had."

So it wasn't his smarts or his knowledge that brought the company down. Instead, he failed for many of the same reasons I've presented in this book. He failed because he had not built a culture that *attended* to what was vital to making the vision a reality, while inhibiting everything else. He had not focused on building an organization characterized by a healthy and positive emotional climate, a connecting culture, optimistic thinking, and the empowerment of individuals in ways that would create strong teams and drive results. He had only focused on the "plan" and the "business" and had expected everything to "just work." He had forgotten that it is always, always, *all* about the people, not just the plan.

But as that story illustrates, and as we saw in the beginning of the book, far too many people think plenty about the plan and not enough about the people.

My hope is that you do not fall into the same trap. I hope that as you have read this book, you have taken a journey toward appreciating how important culture is and how important it is that you start to use these specific boundaries as an essential leadership tool for creating an organization filled with smart people who will thrive. I hope I've been able to convince you that just because you have smart people and a good plan doesn't mean you will succeed. Those are necessary conditions, but they will never be sufficient. It takes more than that.

It is going to require you to accept that you are ridiculously in charge and that you are responsible for establishing the climate for success, setting the terms and expectations for performance with your people, for your organization, and for yourself. You have hired smart people, right? And you have a great plan, right? What could possibly go wrong? The only thing that could get in the way is the failure to *create a culture where brains can flourish, where people are inspired and empowered to do their very best work.*

The good news is that there is a lot you can do to create exactly this kind of culture. Remember, you get what you create and what you allow. There is a lot you can do to create a place where people love to work—and where you do, too. You can choose the kind of place you want to build. You can take charge and lead if you:

> Help people attend to what is important, inhibit what is not important or toxic, and remember what they are doing.
>
> Create an emotional environment that is free of the wrong kinds of stress.
>
> Build teams that are deeply connected.
>
> Help people to think optimistically and root out pessimism.
>
> Help people get in control of what they can control.
>
> Build great teams that are high performance.

Lead yourself in ways that create great performance in others.

Do all of these things, and you will have science on your side. More important, you will have *people* on your side, people who want to work for and with a leader who engenders an environment that attends to our strongest human desires: to connect, create, and grow. You want this for yourself too, and in focusing your attention on it, you make it possible for everyone to win. When you get better, everybody benefits. Be that leader.

I will leave you with one more thought. In my experience, there are three kinds of leaders. First, there is a group that is already very aware of the issues that we have discussed in this book. They are inclined to absorb new ideas and take immediate steps to put these tools to good use. They get help from the inside and outside, and they focus on building positive and empowered cultures. They are constantly seeking feedback and passing along their learning to the rest of their people.

Next, there is a group for whom most of the ideas I've presented here will be entirely new, but they will be open to them. Or perhaps a bit skeptical—not necessarily because the ideas are new to them but because they just haven't seen them implemented very well in the past. But because of their openness they will try them and find out.

Finally, there is a group who will resist the idea that any of this is important; it's all just some sort of psychobabble. Despite the evidence, they tend to believe that working the "plan" is still where it's at. Unfortunately, I don't usually hold out much hope for changing the minds of this third group. They tend to come around only after they have hit the wall and failed.

If you've read this far, my guess is that you belong either to the first or the second group, in which case you already know what to do next: Take charge. Do it. Create an environment and culture where people can be their best. It doesn't have to feel one bit ridiculous if you do it right.

Get ridiculously in charge. Be *that* leader.

Best,
Henry Cloud, Ph.D.
Los Angeles
2013

INDEX

ability, trust and, 183–84, 187
accountability
 control for success and, 145–47
 lack of, and failed teams, 157–59
 trust and, 193–94
action, taking right kind of, 147–49
agendas, and issues of great plan, good people, but poor results, 6
aggression, as human drive, 58–59
Apple Computer
 boundaries on negative thinking, 102
 directly responsible individual, 15
 forward motion, 47
 positive boundaries, 19–20, 26
attention
 behaviors to produce results and, 38–42
 boundaries to encourage, 28–36
 control for success and, 127–28
 executive brain functions and, 27–28
 freedom for creativity and, 42–45
 leadership and, 48–49
 meetings and, 87
 preventing "organizational ADD," 36–37
 tone and self-awareness, 72–74
 transformational moments and, 45–48
 trust and, 167–72
awareness, connection and unity and, 91

behaviors
 changing, to change outcomes, 159–64
 operating values and, 191–92
 trust and, 193, 194–95
"big rocks first" rule, 222–25
blame, and issues of great plan, good people, but poor results, 5
Blanchard, Ken, 63, 205, 206
boundaries
 example of lack of, 6–10
 goals and, xv–xvi
 people's brains and need for, 10–12
 what you create and what you allow, xvi, 14–15, 19, 90, 102, 108, 131, 139, 216, 235
Boundaries (Cloud), xv
brain functions. *See* executive brain functions

"can't be done" virus, negative thinking and, 103–8
capacity and ability, trust and, 183–84, 187
case studies, trust and, 192
cell phones, meetings and, 91
change, self-leadership and acceptance of, 214–16
character, trust and, 180–83
check-in meetings, 88–90
Christensen, Clayton, 101
Clinton, Bill, 96–97
closed versus open systems, self-leadership and, 198–205
Cloud, Olivia, 120–22
coherent narratives, connection and unity and, 92–93
collaboration, connection and unity and, 91–92
communication, importance of common terms and, 160–61
compartmentalized awareness, 91
conflict resolution, connection and unity and, 93–94
connectedness, as operating value, 163
connection
  control and success and, 132–34
  as human drive, 58–59
connection, power through, 77–98
  increased performance and decreased stress, 77–82
  ingredients for, 90–91
  leadership and time together to foster unity and, 84–86
  questions to ask about, 98
  regular meetings to foster, 86–90
  relationships and stress reduction, 82–83
consensus, and issues of great plan, good people, but poor results, 5
control, for success, 125–52
  brain function and, 127–28
  brain slowdown and, 128–31
  "control-divide" exercise, 134–39
  creating connections to deliver program, 132–34
  focusing on what can be controlled, 125–27, 130–31
  positive energy field and, 150–51
  questions to ask, 152
  right kind of actions, 147–49
  structure and accountability, 145–47
  three P's and, 140–45
control and empowerment, defining boundaries and, 16
"control-divide" exercise, 134–39
covenants for behaviors, trust and, 193
creativity, executive brain functions and freedom for, 42–45
credibility, trust and, 180–83
Csikszentmihalyi, Mihaly, 205
culture of organization, 13–14. *See also* emotional climate
  executive brain functions and, 40–42
  importance of, 233–37
  steps in creating of, 235–36
customer intimacy, as operating value, 162, 165
CYA, 56

daily morning meetings, attention and, 30–31, 89–90
"dead fish," team functioning and, 153–54, 157, 161

Death by Meeting (Lencioni), 88–89
delivery, as operating value, 163
denial
  feedback and, 208
  learned helplessness and, 118–19
  self-leadership and breaking through, 227–29
  "worry time" and, 135
direct reports, executive brain functions and, 40–42
directly responsible individual (DRI), 15
disconnection. *See* connection, power through
distractions and diversions, good versus bad, 43
dopamine, brain function and, 108
"dosage," of meetings, 88–90
driver metrics, 194
Dungy, Tony, 125–26, 130–31, 148, 192
Dylan, Bob, 218

e-mail, meetings and, 91
emotional climate, 51–75
  defining boundaries and, 16
  fear as positive motivator, 65–68, 70–72
  goal-oriented behavior and, 57–58
  good pressure and, 63–65
  lower brain and flight-or-fight response, 53–54
  negative and positive emotions, 51–53
  negative tones and triggers, 55–56
  positive consequences and, 68–70
  questions to ask, 74–75
  self-awareness and, 72–74
  tone of communications and, 52–53
  tone while setting boundaries, 58–63
emotional reflection, connection and unity and, 95–96
emotional regulation, connection and unity and, 94–95
emotional repair, connection and unity and, 96
empathy, tone of communication and, 60–61
energy
  open systems and, 199
  self-leadership and rationing of, 225–26
energy field, creating positive, 150–51
execution and goal attainment, executive brain functions and, 39
executive brain function, 25–50
  behaviors to produce results, 38–42
  boundaries to encourage attention, 28–36
  freedom for creativity, 42–45
  leadership and, 48–49
  list of, 27–28, 49
  meetings and, 87
  preventing "organizational ADD," 36–37
  questions to ask, 50
  transformational moments and, 45–48
  trust and, 167–72

fear
  as positive motivator, 65–68, 70–72
  self-leadership and controlling of, 209, 212–13

feedback, self-leadership and, 205–9
stakeholders and, 217–19
weaknesses and, 219–21
fight-or-flight response
emotional climate and, 53–54, 72
self-leadership and feedback issues, 206
"find-a-way" thinking, 120–23
flexibility, executive brain functions and, 39, 49
focus
and issues of great plan, good people, but poor results, 5
strong focus and boundaries, 30–31
weak focus and no boundaries, 31–33

global awareness, as operating value, 162, 164
goal-oriented behavior, emotional climate and, 57–58
goal selection, executive brain functions and, 38–39, 49
Google, 43, 47
guidance, open systems and, 199

high-performance teams, 153–66. *See also* teams
changed behaviors and changed outcomes, 159–64
failed team functions and, 154–56
operating values and, 161–64
operating values and results, 164–66
questions to ask, 166
shared purpose and goals of, 155, 165–66
troubleshooting of troubled team, 157–59

inhibition, executive brain functions and, 27–28
behaviors to produce results, 38–42
control for success, 127–28, 136
freedom for creativity, 42–45
leadership and, 48–49
meetings and, 87
preventing "organizational ADD," 36–37
transformational moments and, 45–48
trust and, 167–72
initiation and persistence, executive brain functions and, 38–39, 49
Innovator's Dilemma, The (Christensen), 101
Integrity: The Courage to Meet the Demands of Reality (Cloud), 178, 182
intent, trust and, 178–80, 187
investments, trust and, 186–87
Isaacson, Walter, 102
isolation, self-leadership and avoidance of, 198–205
iTunes, 102

Jobs, Steve, 19–20, 102

King, Martin Luther Jr., 119
Kotter, John, 216

law of cause and effect, learned helplessness and, 109
law of leadership, 197–98
leaders, three kinds of, 236
leadership. *See also* self-leadership
boundaries and goals, xv–xvi
as discipline, xiii, xiv
law of leadership, 197–98

motivation or demotivation, xiv
people's brains and, xiii–xv
positive and negative energy and, 3–4, 17–18
learned helplessness, 108–16
law of cause and effect and, 109
three P's and, 112–16
Learned Optimism (Seligman), 100
Lencioni, Patrick, 88–89
listening, connection and unity and, 96–97
logging, taking control of three P's and, 140–45

Manning, Eli, 210
mediocrity, and issues of great plan, good people, but poor results, 5
meetings
to foster connection and unity, 86–90
and issues of great plan, good people, but poor results, 5
organizing for attention, 33–35
memory. *See* working memory, executive brain functions and
Metherell, Mark, 120, 183
Metropolitan Life Insurance Company, 100
monkeys, connection and stress reduction study, 82–83
monthly strategic meetings, 89
morale, and issues of great plan, good people, but poor results, 5
morning meetings, attention and, 30–31
motivation, trust and, 178–80
multitasking, 37
mutual awareness, connection and unity and, 91

narratives, connection and unity and, 92–93
Necessary Endings (Cloud), 207, 229–30
negative emotional climate, 51–53
bad stress and, 65
stress and, 55–56
negative energy, 3–4, 17–18
boundary-setting and, 18–21
and issues of great plan, good people, but poor results, 4
negative thinking, 99–123
auditing own thinking, 116–17
auditing team's thinking, 117–20
"can't be done" virus, 103–8
"find-a-way" thinking, 120–23
learned helplessness and, 108–16
questions to ask, 123
setting boundaries on, 99–102
negative thinking, reversing
"control-divide" exercise, 134–39
creating connections to deliver program, 132–34
right kind of actions, 147–49
structure and accountability, 145–47
three P's and, 140–45
neuroscience insights, xiv–xv, 21, 26, 37, 44–45, 128
nonverbal cues, connection and unity and, 91

observation
emotional reflection and, 95–96
taking control of three P's and, 140–45

observing ego
attention and, 73
building of, 60
meetings and, 87
observing structure, trust and, 194–95
off-site meetings, to foster connection and unity, 86–87
One-Minute Manager (Blanchard), 63
open versus closed systems, self-leadership and, 198–205
operating values
building talents, 163–64
communicate to understand, 161
connectedness, 163
customer intimacy, 162
defining to drive results, 164–65
delivery, 163
global awareness, 162
trust and, 191–92
urgency of the vital, 161–62
organizational ADD, avoiding, 36–37
outcomes, self-leadership and not defining self by, 209–11
outside inputs, self-leadership and openness to, 198–205
ownership, as central principle of boundaries, 16–18

past experience, tone of communication and, 61–63
patterns
masquerading as problems, 226–30
as repetition of same work, 230
performance and development, defining boundaries and, 16
"permanent," negative thinking and, 112–16
auditing own thinking, 112–16, 117–20
self-leadership and, 211
taking control of, 140–45
persistence and initiation, executive brain functions and, 38–39, 49
"personal," negative thinking and, 112–16
auditing own thinking, 116–17
auditing team's thinking, 117–20
self-leadership and, 211
taking control of, 140–45
"pervasive," negative thinking and, 112–16
auditing own thinking, 112–16, 117–20
self-leadership and, 211
taking control of, 140–45
Phelps, Michael, 228
planning and organization, executive brain functions and, 38–39, 49
plans
great plan, lack of boundaries example, 6–10
and issues of great plan, good people, but poor results, 4–6
people and success of, 1–3
people's brains and need for boundaries, 10–12
positive and negative energy and, 3–4
positive consequences, 68–70
positive emotional climate, 51–53
goal-oriented behavior and, 57–58
good stress and, 65–68
positive energy, 3–4, 17–18
boundary-setting and, 18–21
positive energy field and, 150–51
power. *See also* connection, power through

and issues of great plan, good people, but poor results, 5
transformational moments and executive brain function, 45–48
powerlessness. *See* learned helplessness
purpose (shared), connection and unity and, 90
pressure, emotional climate and good, 63–65

quarterly offsite meetings, 86–87, 89, 223
questions to ask
about being "ridiculously in charge," 23
about connection, 98
about control for success, 152
about emotional climate, 74–75
about executive brain function, 50
about high-performance teams, 166
about negative thinking, 123
about self-leadership, 231–32
about trust, 196

reality consequences, positive and negative stress and, 67–70
refuting, taking control of three P's and, 140–45
relational consequences, 65–66, 70–71
relevant narrative, connection and unity and, 92–93
repetition
attention and, 28
self-leadership and patterns of, 229–30
review meetings, quarterly, 86–87, 89, 223
"ridiculously in charge," 13–23
clarity from boundaries, 22
culture and, 13–14, 235
focus and energy to realize vision, 18–21
ownership and defining of boundaries, 16–18
people's brains and, 21–22
questions to ask about, 23
self-leadership and, 230–31
"right kind of action," 147–49

seagull management, 63–65
self-awareness
auditing own thinking, 117–20
executive brain functions and, 40–42
tone of communication and, 60–61, 72–74
self-leadership, 16, 197–232
acceptance of change, 214–16
energy and, 225–26
fear and, 209, 212–13
hunger for feedback, 205–9
law of leadership and, 197–98
openness to outside inputs, 198–203
outcomes and, 209–11
patterns as problems, 226–30
patterns as repetition, 230
personal weaknesses and, 219–21
questions to ask, 231–32
stakeholder feedback and, 217–19
staying "ridiculously in charge," 230–31
time audit and, 221–25
self-regulation
emotions and connection, 94–96
executive brain functions and, 49
Seligman, Martin, 100, 108, 112

Sense of Urgency, A (Kotter), 216
shared narratives, connection and unity and, 92–93
shared objectives, 189–91
shared purpose, connection and unity and, 90
speed, and issues of great plan, good people, but poor results, 5
stakeholder feedback, self-leadership and, 217–19
strategic meetings, monthly, 89
stress
  connections to reduce, 77–83
  emotional climate and, 53–56, 59
  positive emotional climate and good stress, 65–68
structure, control for success and, 145–47

tactical meetings, weekly, 89
talent building, as operating value, 163–64
talents, and issues of great plan, good people, but poor results, 4
teams. *See also* high-performance teams
  executive brain functions and, 40–42
  self-leadership and feedback from, 219–21
templates, open systems and, 199
thinking and beliefs, defining boundaries and, 16
three P's, of thinking, 112–16
  auditing own thinking, 116–17
  auditing team's thinking, 117–20
  self-leadership and, 211
  taking control of, 140–45
time audit, self-leadership and, 221–25
tone, while setting boundaries, 52–53, 58–63
  empathy and, 60–61
  past experience and, 61–63
  pressure and, 63–65
track record, trust and, 184–86, 187
transference, authority figures and, 61–63
transformational moments
  adaptation and, 46
  customers and, 47–48
  forward motion and, 47
  growth of people and, 46–47
  power and, 45–46
  results and, 46
trust, 167–96
  accountability systems and, 193–94
  agreeing upon definition of, 173–87
  capacity and ability and, 183–84, 187
  case studies, 192
  covenants for behaviors, 193
  credibility and character, 180–83
  defining trust, 189
  executing of, and performance, 188–95
  executive brain functions and building of, 167–72
  investments and, 186–87
  motivation and intent and, 178–80
  observing structure and, 194–95
  operating values and behaviors, 191–92
  questions to ask, 196
  shared objectives and, 189–91

track record and, 184–86
understanding and, 173–77, 187, 189

understanding
communication and, 161
trust and, 173–77, 187, 189
unity and connectedness, defining boundaries and, 16
urgency of the vital, as operating value, 161–62

vision and strategy
defining boundaries and, 16
executive brain functions and, 40–42
need for focus and energy, 18–21
trust and, 190

weakness, self-leadership and recognition of, 219–21
weekly tactical meetings, 89
what you create and what you allow, xvi, 14–15, 19, 90, 102, 108, 131, 139, 216, 235
working memory, executive brain functions and, 27–28
behaviors to produce results, 38–42
boundaries to encourage attention, 28–36
control for success, 127–28, 136
freedom for creativity, 42–45
leadership and, 48–49
meetings and, 87
preventing "organizational ADD," 36–37
transformational moments and, 45–48
trust and, 167–72
worry time, scheduling, 135

ABOUT THE AUTHOR

Dr. Henry Cloud has been a highly sought-after clinical psychologist and leadership consultant for CEOs and companies for more than twenty-five years, bringing a unique focus encompassing an expertise and understanding of how people perform and relate. He is in demand on many national networks as a speaker and media contributor, and has written numerous books, including *Integrity*, *Necessary Endings*, *9 Things You Simply Must Do to Succeed in Love and Life*, and *Boundaries*, among others. He lives in Los Angeles, California.

www.drcloud.com